SHOW TRANS

Monday

Wow! You very impressive trans! Very handsome!)))

11:49 PM

Today

4:43 PM

I'm a show trans.

2

Show Trans

A Nonfiction Novel By Elliott DeLine

PREFACE:

This preface was originally typed on my phone and scribbled in my personal journal while I sat in a Santa Cruz cafe. I've been out west for about two months now, and today is my last day before I fly out of San Francisco and back to Syracuse, New York. My laptop has been busted for about a week, but today I went with my housemate Lucas to San Jose State, where I'm using a library computer. I've finally got a keyboard in front of me. I've been going insane. Never has it been clearer to me how much I rely on writing for my sanity and on technology to be a writer. At the same time, writing the majority of this by hand gave me time to take pause in a way that was very soothing and useful to my purposes. As I find myself venturing into more personal territory, without the veil of fiction, I need to be careful not to be too impulsive. Not just for my own sake, but that of my readers as well. I want to avoid over-sharing and stick to that which I feel may be relevant to strangers. At the same time, I am seeking a new freedom from self-censorship and shame. You can only write about secrecy for so long – eventually you've got to write about the secrets. It is my hope that perhaps people who are harbouring similar secrets will breathe a sigh of relief in knowing it isn't just them. But as I am one of these people, I also anxiously tear at my hair, wondering, absurdly, if it is in fact just me.

I've never hesitated to be blunt about most things. I never have succumbed to a fear of what the cis or trans public may think of my writing, and for this I've sometimes been criticized. For instance, in 2011, some feared my tongue-in-cheek essay in *The New York Times* would be misunderstood. There are things I have written and completely meant at the time, only to question later on. That's how it goes. I'm not concerned about it.

However, there are two things about which I've always felt the need to be coy: my sexuality and my loved ones. These are of course interrelated. And yet I find myself driven to write about both lately. This trip to the San Francisco Bay Area provided me with some challenges that made me re-examine my ethics as a writer, as well as my responsibility to friends, to other trans people, to myself and to my artistic visions. My nonfiction writing especially, though unpublished, has caused rifts in my personal life. Fictional characters based on people are one thing, and that's lost me a friend or two. But nonfiction writing is razor-sharp. If someone feels you got them wrong...or worse, right...

It's still something I'm trying to figure out.

But as far as writing about sex, I believe I am ready to take some risks. I fear most that I will hurt my family. In fact, if you are my family, I can't help but ask you talk to me before reading the following novel or really anything I've written, ever. But I can't control that. And well, if you haven't disowned me by now...

Despite my anxieties, upon returning to Syracuse, I feel more assured in my work as a writer and dare I say – oh god, do I really dare say? – my work as a reluctant activist. Other people may not quite see what I'm doing. But I think, looking back, it will be coherent. And if nothing else, perhaps I validated some very lovely human beings, "with loves and hates and passions just like mine."

In short: You can't please everyone, so you might as well please yourself. You can't speak the truth, so you might as well speak your truth, and accept, sooner rather than later, that it's going to be a lonely ride.

Part One

I dragged Gabe to the local gay bar in downtown Syracuse. There was a triad of them: Trexx, Rain and Twist. Gabe hates bars, and so do I, but we had to do something, didn't we? We were both depressed beyond belief, stuck living with our parents, and besides, it was New Years' Eve. At the time, Gabe was sleeping with some pudgy (allegedly smelly) kid whom he called Pasty.

"Why Pasty?" I had asked.

"Cuz the muthafucka's pasty!"

Gabe seemed to hate him. They had argued on the phone most of our drive. Pasty didn't like that his boyfriend was going out to a gay bar with another man on New Year's Eve. Gabe tried to explain that we were practically brothers, and had known one another since the eighth grade. But that only seemed to make matters worse.

"In a last ditch effort, I told him you're trans," Gabe said as we walked down the sidewalk, closing his phone.

"Why?" I asked, hiking up the collar of my black pea coat. In the winter, Gabe and I often matched, in our black pea coats, dark, slim-fit jeans, and black boots.

"I thought it would get him off my back. I'm sorry. You know I don't discriminate, but I figured it would shut him up for good."

I smirked. "Okay. I understand." Whatever.

Outside the bar, I saw a man waving. I didn't remember his name, but he always wore a baseball cap. He called me Harry Potter. Several of them do. That or Justin Beiber. I have a remarkable ability to morph into pop culture icons. He would assure me not all older men are creeps, rub my back, tell me I was a good kid for staying in school. He bought me Yuenglings, lit my cigarettes... He reminded me of an uncle I never had. A creepy uncle who was trying to get into my pants, but you take what you can get at times like this.

"Harry Potter!" Baseball Cap yelled, grinning, "So good to see you man!" He was dressed in a tuxedo, but still wearing that awful baseball cap. We embraced. I don't know why.

"Happy New Year," I said. "Nice suit." It really wasn't remarkable, but it seemed the appropriate thing to say.

"Thanks!"

"This is my friend Gabe."

Baseball Cap shook Gabe's hand but didn't really seem to care, because Gabe is Filipino. Most men around here aren't "into" Asians. Baseball Cap looked perplexed for a second. Perhaps he expected Gabe's name to be Chang or something. He then moved his eyes back to my Anglo-Irish features. There are no Filipinos in Harry Potter, as far as I know. No transsexuals either, but my pretend gay uncle didn't yet know that about me. Sure, I was too fem for a lot of gay guy's taste, but I didn't wear my main disclaimer on my face. Gabe sometimes resented me for that. I could feel it.

"Hey, come here," Baseball Cap said, putting his arm around my shoulder. "In case I don't see you again tonight, here's some cash." He pressed two twenties forcefully in my palm. "Have a great night, okay? Here's a pack of cigarettes too. Seriously, have a great night.

You're young, you gotta enjoy it while you can. Dance, have fun, live a little for once! You deserve it."

"OK," I said. "Thanks."

"YOLO!"

"Right."

Gabe sighed as we walk away. "Be careful…"

"I am."

"Ew. He's pointing you out to people!"

"He is?"

"Yeah, to those drag queens."

I looked over my shoulder. I recognized one of the drag queens as someone I had once drunkenly told I was trans. She was black, stocky, shorter than the others, with a tight black dress and high heels. Her make-up and hair were less outrageous than the others. Maybe she was a trans woman. I wondered if she remembered I was transgender and if she would tell Baseball Cap. I didn't much care. It would make things more interesting. Who knows- sometimes it even made me more desirable.

I put the forty dollars in my wallet. Potency.

We entered Rain and sat down by the mirrors, beside an aging lesbian couple in cowboy hats. While Gabe went to the restroom, I thought about the two twenties burning hot in my wallet and admired my own reflection. The environment was too tame though. I had a small taste, and I was craving more.

~~~

We didn't last long at Rain. By eleven, we had smoked all Gabes's cigarettes, he was yawning and checking his phone, and so I drove him home. After I dropped him off, I decided to finally meet up with Michael. I parked my car in the lot off Westcott Street and walked to Taps—a real dive bar, hole-in-the-wall if I ever saw one. It was nondescript and one could easily overlook it. In fact, I had for months, but a Gabe had pointed it out a few days prior, saying, "Hey, did you know there was a bar there?"

In the entranceway, I showed my ID to a man on a barstool, hoping he wouldn't ask why it said I was female. "Mistake," I'd mumble, simultaneously ashamed of myself for being a freak and for being ashamed and considering myself a freak in the first place. The man didn't notice, or at least didn't comment.

I sat at the bar, out of place. A few patrons were punks, huddled at a table in the back, but most the people at the bar were blue-collar, non-descript white men, with one exception—a black guy, homeless or close to it from the looks of his clothes, was entertaining them loudly and wildly with a drunk story. The white men thundered with appreciative laughter. A football game was on the TV.

I ordered a pint of Guinness, and then another, gulping them at record speed due to nerves. I texted Michael under the table, telling him I was here. He said he'd be there any minute.

A few minutes later, I looked up from my Guinness and saw a tall black man's reflection in the mirror across from the bar. He had muscular arms— a linebacker's build— and I was instantly and strongly attracted to him. That's something rare for me to experience. He was wearing a t-shirt that said NAVY and the kind of sunglasses you'd expect someone to wear on a jetski. He wore the same glasses and shirt in the picture he had emailed me. It was definitely Michael.

I caught his eye and we both nodded. I spun around and stood up, shaking his hand jovially as if we were old pals. I could feel the other men looking at us—we were undoubtedly an odd pair. Michael stood about half a foot taller and was probably at least twice my weight. I couldn't hold his gaze for long, and only felt more anxious when he removed his sunglasses to reveal his dark eyes

He insisted on buying me another drink, so I sipped on a Corona with lime, despite that I'd reached my limit. We sat in the back, parallel to the punks.

Michael was (surprise) in the NAVY. Many men online said they were in the military—whether it's true I don't know. Syracuse is close to Fort Drum. He filled me in on all the missions and jargon and training. Having a change in heart, he was now going to nursing school. He wanted to save lives instead of ending them, he said.

It turned out he had previously been in a relationship with a trans woman, but never a trans man. I guess I misunderstood his response to my ad. He said wanted to experience it. It fascinated him. I drank faster.

"So what do you do?" Michael asked, changing the topic.

I said I worked at a library and was a writer. He laughed. "So you're like a librarian?"

"Yeah. Kind of."

"And what, you write like, magazines?"

"No, fictional things. Books."

He laughed again. "Like mysteries?"

"Not really." I started to explain but Michael cut me off to swear at the referee on television. Many of the men in the bar did the same. The punks glared at them.

Michael turned back, but didn't seem interested in continuing the conversation. He took off his hat and scratched his bald head. He then told a long, involved story about his time spent in Tijuana, pausing only to buy me a mix drink that I didn't ask for. "You have to gulp it fast!" It was red, white and blue and tasted like a popsicle.

"It was fun, but I don't recommend it," he said of Tijuana, "a man will get beat with a bat in the streets, and the cops will sit and watch. I've seen it happen. They just sit and watch."

I drove the car home on Michael's suggestion, despite how intoxicated I'd become. It was an extraordinary machine, with built in GPS navigation and satellite radio. I'd never driven a really nice car before, and was surprised how much fun I was having. We opened up the sunroof and cracked the windows. We cruised down the dark city streets, talking and enjoying ourselves.

Michael then asked if I was born female. Surprised by this, I responded yes. That had been in my ad... and I thought I had just explained.

"What surgeries did you have?" Well, that was in my ad too, but I explained my chest and the way testosterone injections masculinized my body.

"Well whatever you do works, because you're really cute," Michael said, groping my inner thigh. It made me blush.

"What is the rudest or most ignorant thing anyone ever asked you?" he asked.

"Um." I thought about it a second. "Well, I had a friend once in high school. I told him I was going to transition, and he asked if I would take pills and grow a penis. That was probably the stupidest question I've gotten."

Michael laughed. "I feel for you. When I was in 9th grade, I was literally the only black kid at my school in Cazenovia. Some kid asked me if black man sperm was the same as white man sperm. So I messed with him and told him mine was purple. And he believed me too." He laughed.

"Wow." I laughed harder than I would have sober. I was warming up to Michael. I wanted his hand back on my thigh. I found I often fell in love briefly and intensely while in moving vehicles.

We made out on his bed in the dark. My jeans were riding up on me unpleasantly. Drunk and free, I removed them, my tee shirt, and my underwear, grinning. Michael raised his eyebrows and grinned as well.

In my memory, there is a blank space here.

I sat on the toilet, naked, but nothing happened. I couldn't pee. Minutes passed and I began to sober up. I realized he wasn't using a condom. I also realized I was really sore and wanted to go home. I headed back in the bedroom.

"Do you wanna ride me?" Michael was barely visible in the dark.

"I'm going home," I said.

"But I didn't make you cum…"

"Did you cum?"

"No."

Thank God. I pulled on my clothes.

Michael sighed and got dressed as well. "I'll drive you to your car."

~~~

"No one is available on Mondays," the receptionist said. She was a stout woman, with curly grey hair and glasses. Probably a volunteer.

"But you're called AIDS Community *Resources*…" I said, with obvious attitude, "there has to be someone I can see."

"Not til next week. And…" she checked a calendar, "All appointments look booked."

"Is there somewhere else I can go? A number I can call?"

"Well, they do STD testing at the County Health Center, but I don't know when. Here's the number."

She begrudgingly handed it over, avoiding the touch of my hand.

I sat in my car with my cell phone to my ear.

"Hello?"

"Hi there. ACR in Syracuse told me you could possibly give me a free STD test?"

"No, I'm sorry, those are only on Thursdays," the man said, "And we aren't doing them this week. We'll be at the ACR building in Syracuse next week to perform them."

"That's where I am now. They said they're booked next week."

"Oh. I'm sorry. Well, good luck to you sir. Try for the following week."

How in god's name was I supposed to wait that long? "Is there nowhere I can go? I'll travel if I have to."

"Well, there's Civic Center in Syracuse. They do free testing daily. Rapid Response tests are every Wednesday, noon to three."

I ended the call, annoyed. No one was going to tell me that?

I drove right down the road, less than a mile, to the Civic Center.

I walked up to a kiosk where a young woman was sifting through papers. She ignored me.

"Hi," I finally said, "Could you tell me–"

"You want room eight," she said, giving me a slightly disgusted look up and down.

"Excuse me? I–"

"STD testing, room eight," she said, gesturing at a pair of teenage girls laughing and chatting as they headed down the hall. "Follow them."

I sat in room eight, filling out the forms. I left my gender blank until the end. I eventually decided to make my own box. Next to it, I wrote "FTM" and put a check mark. I then returned the forms and received a number.

I sat in a blue plastic chair, avoiding eye contact with the mostly female occupants of the room, some with small children. The walls were covered in posters about abstinence. Tables were covered with pamphlets on every STD and drug under the sun, written in English and Spanish. I picked up one. "Do not have sex! It is the only sure way not to get Chlamydia." A cheesy, patronizing video—the kind one would watch in Health class—played in a loop on the television.

I texted Michael.

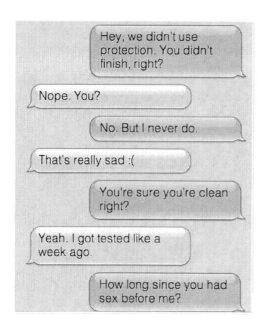

I pressed send just as the nurse called my number.

"So I'll take a swab from the tip of your penis..." the nurse said, filling out a blue sheet of paper. We were seated in a small doctors' room. She was short, thin, probably in her mid-fifties, but looked older.

I blushed. "Oh, I'm...well...Have you heard of transgender?"

The woman stared for a while before responding. "Yes?"

"Well I am that. Female-to-male. So I have a…vagina?"

She bit her lip, thinking. "So are you female or male?"

"Well, I…have a…vagina." Awkward pause. "I was born female."

"So you're a female." She rolled her eyes, ripping up the sheet and grabbing a new, pink one, with a drawing of ovaries and fallopian tubes. "From now on, save us time and put that on the sheet, otherwise we have to start all over. It said you were male."

"I put that I was FTM. That stands for female-to-male."

"Well, they crossed that out and checked male for you because of how you look."

"Oh."

"In that case, you'll need to get undressed."

Each crank hurt like hell. I'd learned to just dissociate in these kinds of situations. And when she scraped something deep with a large cue tip, the shooting pain brought back memories of the previous night. How bizarre, to hold this pose again so soon under such different circumstances. It made the sex seem invasive in retrospect.

"Alright, we'll have some results on Wednesday. Then it'll be another 3 months before HIV would show up."

"Thank you."

"And remember, put female on medical forms." She loomed over me like a threat. "Until you have a penis, you're a female. Got it?"

~~~

A few weeks later I was bored and on Craigslist again. Someone had posted an ad that caught my eye. "LOST CAUSE" it said. I clicked.

There was a picture of Michael. The ad said:

> BE CAREFUL THERE ARE GUYS ON HERE WHO WANNA GIVE PEOPLE HIV ON PURPOSE I SLEPT AROUND AND NOW I FOUND OUT I HAVE HIV I CANT SAY FROM WHO BUT BE CAREFUL!!!

I emailed the anonymous address.

> *-Did we hook up? Is that your picture in the ad?*
>
> *-No, but that's the guy who gave me HIV!!! he's sick and does it on purpose. HELP THE COMMUNITY, STOP HIM FROM SPREADING DISEESE!!*

I winced and closed out of the window. It seemed like a lie. It was probably a vengeful ex, or someone who'd been rejected, or just some psycho starting shit.

I texted Michael.

> Um…did you see the post on Craigslist about you? You might wanna check it out…

> That's my ex. I'm suing him for libel yeah. Can you help me out and tell me the email address he's using? He's been hacking into my facebook too and telling my friends I have AIDS.

> OK. I believe you, but will you please come get tested with me? I don't know you.

I dont believe this is bullshit. I really liked u and it takes something like this to get you to text me?

I said it was a one time thing. I'm sorry, I had no idea you were hurt.

Well I really like u

-Listen I wont know my HIV results til September. Can you go with me to the civic center just to get the rapid-result test? Just to ease my mind? Takes 10 min.

I have work and school I cant just drop everything

Please. anytime. I'll skip work if I have to.

This is bullshit. I hate gay men. This is why I stuck with women for awhile, I dont need this drama.

So you won't go?

I got the test results right on my desk! I'm clean alright?

Can I drive over and see it?

My eyes welled up with tears. I could hear the word *nice* in my head, like frat boys over beers in some porno. "So I totally nailed her. She had such a tight pussy man. I destroyed that thing." "Nice."

I kicked a pebble into the water. I watched as the circles spread outward like sonic waves and then disappeared.

Closing my eyes and inhaling through my nostrils, the lake air smelled like fish and algae. I removed all my garments, climbed up on the railing, and after a moment's hesitation, leapt into the dark water, feet first.

It was pleasantly cool—not a shock to my system but rejuvenation. I stayed submerged for several seconds, swimming near the rocky bottom. I spread my arms and open palms in a cyclical motion to propel forward. When I reached the sand bar, I came up for air, sputtering like humans always do.

I slicked back my hair and then ran my hands over my chest. It was largely numb, but that wasn't uncommon. My scars were a purplish white. It had only been a year since my surgery. What an ordeal. I still sometimes woke in a sweat, remembering the pain and the drug-induced panic. I knew I needed it, but I hadn't known how much it would change me. It was like an awakening. For the first in my life, I felt my body was sexually desirable. Such a realization was messing with my head. I didn't know how to store that knowledge.

My lower half was still submerged. I looked at it, glowing whitish green beneath the water. The rest wasn't visible to me without a mirror. It was only really seen by others.

"Nice."

I did a shallow dive and swam some more. Soon my mind went blank. I felt wonderfully alive and at peace, the way I imagine many people do making love. It was the first time I'd ever done this naked, and there seemed almost a symbolic, baptismal quality.

There was no one in sight, so I stood up in the shallows. I rested my hands on my glowing white ass and leaned my head back, looking up at the stars. The Syracuse pollution dimmed them, but out here in Cicero, further north of the city, it was a regular planetarium. I closed my eyes, content.

I resented the possibility of more doctors, medications, stigmas, and secrets. More questions of disclosure and reasons to be untouchable. An early death.

Yet there I was, knee deep in the lake water, smiling and wiggling my toes. I watched the mini, underwater sand storms stir up and then settle once more. I wasn't afraid. My body was something miraculous and self-healing, like a starfish. It wasn't teen-like impudence. I knew in my soul I would never wither.

I remembered our naked bodies pressed together. The rhythm. The strange and wonderful feeling of his entry, before the sobering pain.

Come what may. I regretted nothing.

~~~

He wanted to know my name. Sometimes I've just lied, but I tonight I told him the truth for some reason. I wonder if he remembered even a second after I told him. He didn't tell me his. After we entered his small, floor-level apartment, we were engulfed in artificial light. I noticed the whites of his eyes were bloodshot. Though I couldn't smell anything, I suspected he was high. I tried to look him over without being too noticeable. I found there was something very familiar about him. He was about my height and athletic—more muscular than I am, with a buzz cut. Blonde hair, blue eyes, attractive. And yet the arousal from the reckless, liberating car ride to a stranger's apartment had passed. He reminded me of high school, I realized. Not one boy in particular—he just resembled my memories of boys from that time. A more grown-up version of the jocks who laughed at me. I just felt nervous.

"So I don't really do this," he said as I slipped off my shoes, avoiding his gaze, "How do we start?"

I put my wallet and my car keys on a glass coffee table and sat on the plush sofa. "Well, I'm not sure. I'm not drunk, so I'm a little awkward." I followed this with a *heh* noise of self-deprecation. He stayed standing.

"Do you have a bedroom or something?" I asked.

"Oh," he said, "Yeah. This way." He led me down the wall to a room with a queen-sized bed with a taupe comforter. I walked right in, trying to build up confidence, and sat on the right side of the bed. I noticed a picture of him and his girlfriend on the mantle above the bed. They were dressed up, going to a prom or something of the like. She was big, curvy, Italian looking, and pretty.

"Let me get my cell phone just in case she calls," he said. He must have noticed my gaze. The unnamed girlfriend got out of work at 9:30. It was 8:00 when I parked outside his building. We still had time.

He came back and set his cell phone on the dresser. "So you wanna just like, strip down?" His tone was surprisingly polite. I could tell he saw me as a female.

"I guess so. Sure."

"Alright, and I'll do the same."

"Right." I started to take off my shirt, but stopped. "Have you ever been with a guy?"

"No," he said. "You have, right?"

"Yes."

This changed how I would approach things. There were different types of men who took interest in me, and different protocals I followed accordingly. I put this guy into the category of *pussy is pussy*. Sure there was a homoerotic element, otherwise why me? But mostly, it was pussy he wanted. Possibly my androgynous, slightly curvy and boyish frame excited him. Possibly my ass. But mostly, pussy.

"Can we maybe kill the lights?" I asked, knowing nothing above my waist interested him.

"Oh, you want it to be dark?"

"If you don't mind. Or at least dimmer."

He flipped the switch.

"Oh," I said, thinking it was too dark for a second, then my eyes adjusted. I undressed quickly and lay on his bed on my side.

He was naked too, at the foot of the bed, sitting. "So what do you wanna do?"

I was frustrated, having been relying on him to assert dominance. "Well, I don't want to just start making out with you," I said, "if you're straight and it's gonna weird you out or something, you know?"

He nodded slowly. "Well, do you kiss like a girl?"

I stifled a laugh. "I really don't know. Maybe."

"Hm." He was silent for a few seconds. "I'll get a condom."

"I have one, don't sweat it."

"So should I just go down on you or something? That usually gets me hard."

"Sure, go for it."

I gave him a cold smile as he got on his knees and then stomach and looked up at me—to give him the OK. I nodded.

He didn't give me enough time to even really feel it before he stopped. He just sort of grazed everything with his tongue.

"Wanna sixty-nine?" he asked.

"My mouth is dry," I said, and it was true. I also didn't want to at all.

"Okay." He didn't seem bothered. "Well, did you want to fuck?"

"Yeah." I got the condom, ripping it open incorrectly, and handed it to him. "Here. I don't really know what I'm doing... there," I said. I didn't want to touch him for some reason. He still seemed unruffled.

As soon as he started I was already ready to stop. It just felt like being jabbed with a stick.

"Oh fuck," he said, thrusting and clearly enjoying himself a lot more than I was. "Oh fuck yeah." He repeated this phrase several times. My legs were in the air and over his shoulders. I felt a little ridiculous. I found I was gripping the sheets, though I'm not sure why. I was going to give it a few more seconds, but this really wasn't pleasurable.

He stopped just as I was going to suggest it.

"Will you do it from behind instead?" I asked. I thought we would both appreciate not having to look at one another.

"I came," he said.

"Oh." I laughed. I realized that was rude, and said, "Oh okay, cool. Good."

I rolled over and sat on the edge of the bed, still feeling weird and somewhat outside of my body. I hadn't completely dissociated, but I definitely was not in tune with myself. There was a disconnect - a sort of lag. "Well, I should head out."

"Got somewhere to be?" he said.

"No, but I should really get home."

"OK."

I got dressed as he walked over and flipped on the light. I looked again at the photo of his girlfriend again. I was pretty sure I was done with men for a while. I had a sudden, strange desire to cuddle with her.

"So you can't text me or call me or anything," he said as I headed for the door. He handed me my keys and wallet.

"Don't worry," I said, "I won't even save your number."

He looked relieved. "Well, bye then."

"Yeah. Text me if you ever want to do that again." I wondered why I said that. I didn't mean it, did I?

I walked out to the car, relieved that it was over. I got inside and turned on the engine. It was 8:17. The whole thing had lasted less than twenty minutes. I laughed as I pulled out of the driveway and drove home, driving the memory out of my mind.

~~~

The bartender at Trexx was bald, buff, and wore camouflage pants, but was effeminate in his voice and mannerisms. He was white, and probably in his forties. He usually seemed drunk. He told stupid jokes to the older men and drag queens who sat along the bar in the neon lime green glow of the overhead light. "Hey John, John…John! What do you call a lesbian dinosaur? He'd rub his hands together, grinning and suppressing his giggles. "Give up? A Lick-a-lotta-puss!"

I approached the bar, wishing there was someone to order for me. I always got nervous for some reason. Perhaps it was an automatic reaction born of the days when I was androgynous and subject to cross-inspection. Drunk gay men are not known for their tact. I never knew how much to tip, either.

"Hey you! Long time no see!" He always said this to me. I don't think he knew my name but he definitely knew my face. "What- "

"Hi," I mumbled. I cut him off as he was going to say something else. I'm bad about that when I'm nervous. "I'll have a glass of champagne."

"That's it?"

"Yeah."

"You don't want it mixed with anything?"

"Nope."

"Just on the rocks?"

"Sure," I said, thinking that was a bizarre way to talk about champagne. Was it really that strange to order? I knew it was a mildly eccentric habit, but it was my favorite drink at the time.

"Here you go," he said, handing me a tumbler of golden liquid. "Five dollars." As he turned away, I sniffed it. It was whiskey. I watched him put away the bottle. Jim Beam. He thought I said "a glass of Jim Beam."

I didn't say anything. Whatever, I'd learn to like it.

I squeezed my way through the crowd and the back door. Trexx was always so crowded. So many young people and yet none of them appealed to me. Out behind the bar was a section of concrete. A cheap fence of chain link and wood surrounded it, so that we couldn't see to the main road on the right. You could still see the city buildings, billboards, and highways up above it. There were a couple booths and picnic benches, all occupied. People stood or sat in mixed-gender clusters, smoking. I stood alone. I was glad to still have some of the cigarettes that Baseball Cap gave me on New Years, even if they were menthol.

There was a young man on my right who was also alone. I eyed him stealthily, pretending to look over his head towards the door. He wore a brown leather jacket and sort of had a similar style to my own. He was white and slim, with handsome chiseled features, scruff, and dark, shaggy hair. Not my usual macho type, but someone I could appreciate as handsome. He struck me as Russian- or at least somebody who enjoyed Russian literature. There aren't a lot of people who look like that in Syracuse. I sipped some nasty liquid courage, then said, "Hey," nodding at him.

He nodded back but didn't smile and then continued to focus on his cigarette.

"I guess we're both wallflowers," I said.

He raised his eyebrows and half-smirked without looking at me. It was not a friendly expression. It was a "You're awkward," expression. I decided not to push it.

I noticed a heavy blonde woman staring at me from one of the booths. I pinched my nose and gulped some more of the whiskey. Disgusting. I screwed up my face and shuddered. For a second I thought I might heave it back up, but then I was fine. I set the drink down on the pavement before heading back towards the door. I wasn't going to finish it.

Back inside, I found a seat in the back lounge room, beside one of those claw machines and a photo booth. I sat down on the faux-suede loveseat, checking my phone. Though we hadn't seen each other in years, or exactly ended things on good terms, I found myself texting Isaac when I was drunk at a gay bar. I was waiting for his response to my oh-so important message:

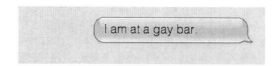

I looked up from my phone and saw that same blond woman was again looking at me and coming closer. She had a circular, pale face framed by straight, bleached hair that came about to her ears. She was fat and femme, with earrings, make-up, pink skirt, the whole nine yards. She had several beaded rainbow bracelets on her arms. She was a bracelet-girl. Every high school had at least one in the early 2000's. There were a lot of them at Trexx. It was definitely a bracelet-girl kind of place.

"Hello," I said, unable to avoid it any longer.

"Hi sweetie," she said, leaning in. "You're gay, right?"

It was a nosey, leading question, but understandable given the circumstances. "Sort of, I guess. I'm bi. Kind of." I thought queer would sound pretentious. No one in Syracuse used queer. I didn't know if I wanted to, either.

"My friend thinks you're cute," she said. She nodded towards a man at the bar, who she had been standing with outside. He was mildly attractive: olive-skin, hairy, probably Italian or Greek. He wore a red polo that either said Hollister, American Eagle, or Abercrombie & Fitch, and faded, loose fitting jeans. He was dressed like a popular kid dressed when I was in high school. Upstate style lags slightly behind New York City trends. I was undoubtedly falling behind now as well.

I nodded, acknowledging I had heard her.

"Do you think he's cute?" she asked.

I shrugged. I guess that was enough of a go-ahead for him. A few minutes later, the pair of them was gushing over me.

"You are so hot," he said, loudly and gaily, "Do you even know how hot you are?"

"No, he's shy," Claire said. Claire was the blond woman's name. The man's name was Anthony.

"He doesn't even know he's hot, and that makes him even hotter!" Anthony shouted over the music.

They both offered to buy me drinks. Anthony ended up paying. He got me a Long Island Ice Tea. And then a second.

"Drink it, drink it…" he kept urging, getting touchier as the night went on.

It was a College Thursday, which meant there was a drag show on the stage at midnight. Time passed quickly when I drank, and the dance floor was soon packed with people for the show.

I checked my cell phone. There was finally a message from Isaac.

I'm at a gay bar too!! In SF. I danced on a stage to This Charming Man! It made me think of you. You would love it here!!

I laughed to myself. Here they were playing Lady Gaga. And not even the newer stuff.

After I had finished either my second or third mixed drink, I found myself stumbling towards the stage and then climbing upon it. The drag queen hostess, Frita Lay, was calling people up to compete for Virgin of the Night. A virgin was someone who'd never been to Trexx before. I was being deceitful—I had been to Trexx before. I stood amongst the line of giggling, drunk college students—mostly girls, with a few gay friends.

"And who are you, honey?" Frita Lay asked, putting the microphone in my face.

"I'm…Alex," I said, because it was the first name that came to mind. Alex was usually my go-to-fake-name. I'm not sure why. I'm not even that fond of it.

The crowd was somewhat blurry. I heard Frita Lay say something and gesture towards my crotch. Everyone laughed. I was packing: something I only did when going to a gay bar. I'm guessing I either looked well-endowed or erect. Or both. Whoops.

"Are you gay, Alex?"

"No, I'm transgender." I said this into the microphone, looking at her with drunk, drooping eyes. I felt vaguely threatening.

"Oh," she said. "Well, alright, whatever floats your boat."

I could feel everyone staring at me. Anthony and Claire were a few rows back, but I couldn't make out their expressions. I just kind of bobbed my head drunkenly, closing my eyes.

After examining a few others, Frita named me the Virgin of the Night. I won Trexx! I bowed and then hopped off the front of stage.

"I didn't realize you were a transguy," Claire said, now eying me with obvious interest.

"Yep," I said, shrugging with the nonchalance of a true badass.

"Wait, transgender which way?" A man's voice asked me. I didn't see his face.

"Every way," I said. I was ready to leave now. Claire and Anthony wanted to exchange numbers, so we did. I crossed the room and picked up my jacket from the coat check. I forgot to tip.

Outside there was a cool spring breeze. I stuffed my hands in my pockets. Most the buildings nearby were abandoned, except a modern structure that housed the local newspaper company. Upstairs from Trexx there used to be a salon that allegedly shut down because it was a hotbed of STDs. With a shudder of anxiety, I thought of the HIV results I was still waiting on.

An old white car drove past me with its windows down. I glanced upwards.

"My friend thinks you're hot!" a girl's voice yelled.

"OK," I yelled.

"I'm wanna rape your ass!" a man's voice yelled.

"Charming!" I yelled.

I sat in my car for a while, resting in the parking lot. I knew I shouldn't drive but was wondering what else I could do. My phone buzzed.

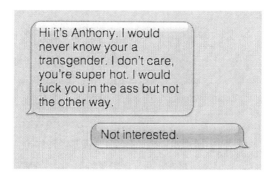

I spoke the words "Not... interested" aloud to myself as I typed them. Then I lay my head on the steering wheel and fell asleep.

Josh zipped up his jeans and stood over me. I still lay on his sofa, zoned out.

"Alright," he said, "Well, I gotta get to bed. I have work in the morning."

I was staring at a large stack of DVDs to my left. He had a rack almost as tall as the ceiling. None of the titles looked remotely interesting. *Wedding Crashers, Batman Begins, Ghostbusters...* "OK," I said, "That's fine. Do you mind if I just lay here for a bit and sober up?"

"Actually I do," he said. "I've got a lot of valuable stuff in here. My Playstation and DVDs...and I don't know you."

I thought this was sort of awful but didn't say anything. "Alright. I'll go somewhere else to sober up."

But by the time I was in the car, I figured I might as well just drive home. It wasn't that far.

I tossed and turned in bed that night as I replayed the events of the night. Josh was pretty plain-looking, with brown hair, eyes, and beard. He had an average, out-of-shape body, and an inoffensive face with red, stoner eyes. He lived in a small, rundown house on the Southside of Syracuse, in the Valley. It was a rougher part of town, near the community college and the Onondaga Nation territory. Although about my age, he was a single dad with two daughters, who were sleeping upstairs while we fucked. He considered himself straight.

"You were in my class at SU," Josh said. "The one about Indian religion or some shit."

It was called Religion and the Conquest of America.

"I couldn't believe it," he said. "I said to the guy next to me, I used to hook up with her."

Her? That must have confused the guy. I had been on hormones over three years at this point and had chest surgery the previous summer. Why hadn't I said something? Anything? Instead I just smiled…

I got up for some water and decided to sit on the couch in the dark. I leaned my chin on my palms and my elbows on my thighs and stared at my bare feet on the wood floors.

Why was I doing these things? My sexuality seemed to me then like a dark forest, full of danger, and despair. I was utterly disoriented. My only compass was…Love. I pulled my cell phone from the pocket of my sweatshirt. Love. Recognition. Affinity.

Despite that he had seriously fucked me over and broken my heart, I had lingering affection for Isaac. It had been several years since I dropped out of Purchase College, suicidal and depressed. For a while I hated him, then I simply became indifferent. But lately, we had been talking a little, and all the old feelings seemed to be reemerging. I knew it was illogical, but I couldn't ever quite let go of the dream. We were two sensitive, artistic, intelligent, troubled trans men, struggling to find our way through the brambles. Like Frodo and Sam, Sherlock and Watson, Robin Hood and Littlejohn. The stuff of which fanfictions are written. But the flamboyant hero needed a practical sidekick more than the practical sidekick ever needed a flamboyant hero. Plus the practical sidekick was cheating on his girlfriend and could be a very cruel bastard indeed.

I wasn't obsessing about it. Only he had written me a facebook message earlier that week.

Isaac

I'm in Italy. I've been climbing and hiking in the Alps. It's beautiful. I find myself thinking about everything. About my college years. About you. I really miss seeing you. I think you'd absolutely love it here. Italian men remind me of you for some reason. I see so many well-dressed, slim guys and for a second I almost think they are you. I think we should try to get together when I come back. Only if you're interested of course. I think it could be nice. You could come to stay in Rhode Island or I could even come to Syracuse if you prefer. After all your stories, I feel like I almost know the place, so I'd be curious to visit. I miss you.

Draw me in, retreat. That was the pattern. I knew this. I had no illusions. It had also been the pattern with Amy, the object of my affection from age twelve to seventeen. Was my past responsible for my present, inexplicable and stupid behaviors? I couldn't even call them desires. Or at least I didn't want to.

During sex, Josh switched to the other orifice. This sudden change caught me off guard. It wasn't that I was necessarily opposed to this, but I thought that he should have asked permission. Maybe I'm wrong- neither of us had talked so far, why start communicating now? I didn't say anything. Instead I drifted off into a reverie of nothingness and despair, doubled by alcohol intoxication. I stayed there, numb, until he finished.

~~~

I sat in the backseat of Gabe's Corolla. Unbeknownst to him or Ian, his work friend in the passenger seat, I was fuming. Ian was a chubby, baby-faced boy from Puerto Rico who Gabe was sort of into. He was pretty fem and not Gabe's usual type. Gabe introduced us on another occasion, but I hardly knew him. From the car ride, I had learned that he had a passion for Miley Cyrus, and that was enough for me to turn up my nose.

The two of them were chattering away about the people they worked with at the call center, and I had nothing to contribute. It was Gabe's birthday, meaning it was to be his night. But early that evening, I was fired from my job at the library. It had come as a real shock and I still didn't understand why, despite my boss's list of my character flaws. I thought I was doing well.

Library clerks are supposed to be paid thirteen dollars an hour. This is considered a living wage by many activists. It is the amount of money a person should make an hour, for forty hours a week, to live comfortably. I looked online once, and most clerks make fifteen—but it's expected we get paid less in a place like Syracuse. As I was technically only a page, I made seven-fifty and worked thirty hours a week. A Bachelor's degree didn't change this. This kept me just below the amount I needed to move out of my parents' house and live my life. It was a job usually reserved for high school kids, and it was a real insult. However, almost every shift that winter, I was asked to work at the desk with the other clerk, Courtney. Marcia had been out sick for several weeks. Instead of hiring a new clerk, my supervisor, Ballard, had given me an unofficial promotion, sans the pay raise. This was something I was beginning to resent, but I was too passive to comment. He hired a new page to do my old job—an auburn haired, chubby teenage girl whose name escapes me.

With about twenty minutes to 9:00, I had noticed that the director, Pat, had stopped in. She rarely did this—I'm not really sure what she did at all, to be honest. I'd only spoken to her once or twice since I was hired. She came up to the desk and flashed me a phony smile. "Elliott, hiii. When you get a moment, come in to my office alright? We need to discuss something."

"Oh, OK," I said, my voice high-pitched and my mouth going dry. "Is everything OK?"

"So just finish up whatever you're doing," she said, "and come on in."

I scanned the barcodes of the remaining books at lightning speed, one beep of the computer after another. I was anxious and wondering what was up. Maybe she was going to mention how I was always late to staff meetings. This was admittedly becoming a problem. I'd apologize and come up with an excuse...or just tell the truth, that I was horrible at estimating the time needed to drive to work. Maybe she wasn't mad. I had been trying extra hard at everything else, mostly out of guilt. Maybe she noticed. If I had any luck, she was going to offer me an official promotion to clerk. Actually, that seemed the most likely, given the timing. I hadn't done anything wrong, at least recently, so there was no reason to feel so nervous.

I knocked on her door at about a quarter of.

"Come in Elliott," she said, "and please close the door."

I did, and then sat across from her at the desk. "So," I said. I waited as she shuffled her papers. She was a thin woman whose age was undeterminable—I'd place her somewhere around my mom's age if I had to guess. She looked like she'd had work done on her face, and her hair was dyed platinum blonde, cut straight and severe. She wore a navy business suit and high-heels with pantyhose.

"Is there a problem?" I asked.

"Well Elliott," she said, using my name yet again, "Yes, there is."

"Oh?" My heart sped up.

"You see, we don't feel you're fitting in well here."

"But I've been here over a year."

"You seem bored with the position. I don't think it's a good fit."

I just stared blankly.

"Wouldn't you agree?" she said. "You seem bored."

"I don't know," I said, "I mean, sure, I get bored sometimes, but that's any job for you. Over all, I'm happy here."

"You don't seem it. You're generally moody and unfriendly."

"I am?" I furrowed my brows. "Honestly, I'm a little shy, but I thought I was doing a pretty good job—"

"There are reports of you using the computers and checking your phone."

"I mean…yeah, I'll admit I did that. I didn't realize it was a big deal. I'm really sorry. Other people were doing it so I thought it was OK. I know that isn't an excuse but— "

"There have been a lot of mistakes in the shelving."

"But I've mostly been up at the desk," I said.

"We've pinpointed the mistakes to the days you are working," she said, ignoring me, and shuffling her papers once more. "You seem unfocused, and attention to detail is crucial when working in a library."

"I don't understand," I said. "I mean, it's possible I've made some mistakes…" My eyes were starting to sting. Don't cry, I told myself. Whatever you do, do not cry…

"You're more of the creative type. Wouldn't you rather just be a writer?"

"I am," I said, "But you can't make a living from that alone. And I like working at a library." Wait, how did she know I was a writer?

"Still, there must be jobs better suited for you," she said.

"Am I being fired?" Tears streamed down my face. I tried to pretend I hadn't noticed.

"Unfortunately, I have no other choice but to let you go," she said. "You can stay in my office until you're composed, then please collect your things and leave."

She got to her feet and left me, humiliated and choking on tears. I tried and failed to get a grip, and it was several minutes before I was able to sneak out the back door, hiding my face. I was completely caught off guard. I felt angry, betrayed, confused, and never more uncertain of my future.

At the bar, Ian and Gabe were busy flirting, barely touching their bottles of hard apple cider. I sat to the side, a third wheel, feeling depressed and anxious. I decided to go throw some darts. Rain was definitely a gay bar, not a club. Even on a Friday, it was pretty deserted. They had moved earlier in year to this new space on the West Side. It was an equally sketchy part of the city. Most the other buildings on the street were boarded up and for lease. Our first night there, someone smashed Gabe's car window. They stole his cigarettes and a duffle bag full of dirty gym clothes. Pretty pointless.

I had recently gotten an iPhone and downloaded the Grindr app. I recognized the irony of sitting in a gay bar, staring at a gay dating app on a screen...but this didn't stop me from doing it. I had been talking with several guys, most of whom did not interest me. But one user, Auburn_jock, somehow had managed to hold my attention, despite that I had never seen his face.

There were several misleading things about Auburn_jock. For starters, he did not live in the neighbouring city of Auburn, but in downtown Syracuse. Also, he was not a jock. The muscular torso in his user picture, I would soon discover, was not him at all. Auburn_jock was just as bad as all the other cis guys online. He texted me,

I don't even care if you don't have a dick, you're really hot! You make a hotter guy than most regular guys lol.

He was traditionally gay, not to mention an idiot. Yet for reasons I still do not entirely understand, I was quickly drinking my glass of spumante and messaging with him. When I discovered he was also at a bar, I persuaded Gabe and Ian to go there, without telling them the reason why.

The bar was called Al's Wine and Whiskey Lounge. It was a popular bar in downtown with plush furniture and a comparatively upscale setting. It was crowded with straight white people. There was a group of dudes playing darts and being loud in the back. Gabe and Ian were absorbed in each other and hardly noticed when I snuck off to the men's room.

From the stall, I texted Auburn_jock.

Where are you?

At Al's. Where are you?

In the bathroom, come find me.

Seriously?

Yeah, the second stall to the right.

OK, coming

I steadied myself, leaning against the wall. This was crazy. But I was drunk enough that I couldn't help myself. I wasn't myself. This wasn't something I did. But I was doing it.

About a minute later there was a knock at the door. I opened it, seeing Auburn_jock face to face for the first time. He moved quickly, pinning me against the wall and shoving his tongue in my mouth. He was a dark, short, hairy type of fellow, overweight, balding, and not at all attractive to me. Was it too late to back out? He undid my pants and peeled down my briefs, exposing my recently-shaved pubis in the fluorescent lighting.

"Wow..." he said, touching my genitals with his fat fingers. He examined the curves and folds with unrestrained, almost violent awe. "Wow. I can't believe that. That is so fuckin hot."

~~~

Gabe drove us home later that night. I lay in the backseat, and I called Isaac on the phone. It was late, so I was surprised he picked up. Then I realized the time difference. But regardless, he shared my phobia of phone calls. "Elliott? What's going on?"

"I had sex with a gross guy," I said. "I need to get away. There are no queer men here. Just gay guys..."

"What's that supposed to mean?" Ian said, glancing back and giving me a catty look.

"It's OK," Isaac said. "What happened, happened. There's no use beating yourself up over it. But are you going to be OK?"

"I don't know," I said. "I feel out of control. I feel possessed or something."

Isaac sighed. "You've gotta get out of that place. It's killing you. Trust me, I've been there. I know exactly how you're feeling. That's why I had to get out of Rhode Island. "

We talked the rest of the drive home, and I only hung up when Gabe pulled into my parents' driveway. Exhausted, I stumbled up the stairs, crawled into bed still in my clothes, and fell asleep almost instantly.

Auburn_jock wanted to keep hooking up after that. The rational part of me did not want that at all, but my irrational side saw an opportunity.

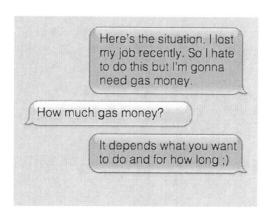

> Here's the situation. I lost my job recently. So I hate to do this but I'm gonna need gas money.

> How much gas money?

> It depends what you want to do and for how long ;)

Isaac and I had started texting one another regularly, just talking about the events of our days. I shared with him with my newfound source of income. I didn't even tell Gabe about that. I wasn't sure what reaction I wanted to get. Mostly I needed to confess and vent to someone I thought could maybe understand. But admittedly, in a twisted way, I thought the tales might make him care for me more. I suspected the sadness of my life was both what attracted him to me and drove him away.

I learned that Isaac had moved out to San Francisco for graduate school. He was getting a Masters in Women and Gender Studies, but he had dropped out after a year. He had also broken up with his girlfriend since we had spoken last. He urged me to come visit him. It'd be good for me to get away, he said. Plus he seemed sad and lonely as well. I mused to Gabe that it was possible he wanted to hook up with me, but I didn't really think so. It seemed we both were just in need of a friend. Besides being transgender, we had often felt a bond when together that was hard to explain. One time I got him to take the Myers-Briggs personality type test and discovered that like me, he was an INFP. Perhaps that had something to do with it. When I let myself, I felt a tremendous attraction to him, in the very sense of the word, as if caught in a magnetic field.

I was published in an anthology that previous fall, and it was nominated for a Lambda Literary Award. It was a collection of transgender short stories. When I discovered there would be an award ceremony in San Francisco, this gave me an excuse to pay four-hundred dollars for a plane ticket. I would fly out in May. When I announced to Isaac that it was official, via text, he didn't respond for about a week. That struck me as strange, but I tried not to take it personally. When he finally did text me, he said.

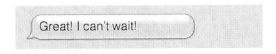

Great! I can't wait!

Neither could I. I hadn't been out west since my childhood, and I hadn't left New York State in years.

The business with Auburn_jock continued, though why I bothered is hard to say. It wasn't much money, and he tried to weasel out of paying every time. He started making excuses such as that he forgot and he only had a twenty on him, or he lost his wallet. My sexual performance, unenthusiastic from the start, continued to decline. Eventually he stopped responding to my texts all together. That was a tad embarrassing, but at the same time, a relief.

I found another gig in Cortland, with a guy named LaxDude007. After several close examinations on webcam, he wanted to see in person. I gave him the "gas money" line as well, and I drove out that weekend to the boonies to collect. Amidst expanses of empty land, cows, and broken telephone wires, I found a tiny house on a dead end street. LaxDude was big, in more ways than one. He let me smoke out of his giant bong and I got so high that it might as well have been morphine. It was a pleasurable sexual experience, but I was entirely alone, unaware of his existence, absorbed entirely in my sensations. Then he gave me fifty bucks and I disappeared.

When I came through, I was driving somewhere in Homer, New York—one of those typical upstate small towns. It was summer, so I pulled over at an ice cream stand on the side of a country road. I sat in the sun at a picnic table, licking the chocolate sprinkles off chocolate ice cream. It tasted amazing. The air was warm and the wheat fields and hills around me were quite beautiful. I felt less than safe but content. I texted Isaac, telling him what I'd just done. Confiding in him made it feel more like I was doing research. It wasn't that it was awful work. It was just terrifying to consider I might be enjoying it. I couldn't make sense of that—despite sex being physically pleasurable, also it felt poisonous. Draining. I often felt ill… Sticky and over-stimulated. Could one be simultaneously asexual and compulsively sexual? I felt out of sync with my sense of self. Why did I do these things? It didn't fit. And there were the memory lapses. Those scared me the most. But I had raised enough money to cover a plane ticket to San Francisco, and for the time being, that was all that mattered. I needed to get away and clear my head. I needed to talk to Isaac.

Part Two

"Please don't touch my crotch," I thought. Maybe he wouldn't notice. Maybe he'd just think I was cold—that I was suffering from 'shrinkage,' as they called in on Seinfeld. Then again, my license in his hand still said "female." Or rather, "F." As in, "faggot," and "fuck you." Why hadn't I changed that yet?

I hate airports and I hate airplanes. I prefer trains, and I'll even take a Greyhound over any form of aviation. But this was the only practical way to get to California for a week.

"Please empty your pockets, sir," the kid said.

I didn't realize I was carrying anything. I dug around and retrieved a St. Jude medal. "Oops." I didn't remember putting that there. I'm not really Catholic, just superstitious and fond of my Irish ancestry. I suppose the patron saint of desperate causes was only appropriate for this particular journey.

The kid nodded. "OK, you're all set."

Breathing a sigh of relief, I moved on to retrieve my luggage and amble on towards the terminal. It was mid-morning on a Friday, and the Syracuse airport wasn't crowded. I bought a cup of mediocre coffee from a shop then sat by the gate and waited in a black leather seat. I listened to music on my CD player until it was time to board.

When I arrived in San Francisco, I took the BART to the Mission District, where Isaac lived. It was cleaner than the New York subway. Before I went underground, Isaac texted me, saying to meet him at the 26th Street station. Surprisingly, I figured out how to get there with ease. I felt pleased with myself. I sat cross-legged, my foot jiggling and my heart pounding. As the doors of the train opened, I saw him standing by the stairs beyond the gates. He was recognizable but had changed. He looked more masculine and mature. Once unable to even grow sideburns, he now had a nearly full-faced reddish brown beard.

He was leaner. He looked less like a cute chubby boy with glasses and more like what I imagine he had always desired.

"Hey!" I said when I was a little closer. I swiped my card once but the gates wouldn't open. I tried again. No luck. I laughed nervously.

"Turn it the other way," Isaac said.

"Right." I swiped the card again and the gates opened. My suitcase was crooked and caught on the side. I had to tug several times. The gates snapped shut on my hips and I let out a yell.

"Here, Elliott..." Isaac strode forward and grabbed the suitcase, lifting it into his arms and setting it off to the side. "Are you OK?" he asked, biting his lip to suppress a smile.

"Yeah, it mostly just startled me," I mumbled.

"How are you?" It wasn't a question, so much as an exclamation. He opened his arms to me and I embraced him.

"I'm well," I said.

"Great," he said, pulling away. "I'm so happy you're here."

"You look so different," I said.

"Do I?"

"Yeah...you've got a beard. And you look older. In a good way."

"I adjusted my hormones a few months ago. They started testing my blood levels at my new doctor's, and it turns out the folks in New York weren't giving me the right dose. Everything is so much better out here. They get that transition isn't a one-size-fits-all kind of thing."

"That's excellent," I said, wondering if my own testosterone levels might be off.

"I feel a lot better," Isaac said. He gestured towards the stairs. We walked up into the light of the streets. I lifted my hand to shade my eyes.

"Wow..." I looked around, caught of guard by all the colors. So many pastels! I always thought the Painted Ladies occupied a single street. But these were entire neighborhoods, full of pink, blue, yellow, purple, and green houses. It was like Westcott Street in Syracuse but a million times more vibrant and alive. And the street art! As we walked down the road, every wall seemed covered in a mural. They featured a tiger, sea lions, famous revolutionaries, rainbows, Our Lady of Guadeloupe… I felt like a child, utterly wrapped up in the excitement of it all.

"There is more street art here," Isaac said, "per square foot, than anywhere in the country."

"Wow." That seemed like it was the only thing I knew how to say. I thought of all the people who had traveled the world to come here. Queer people, trans people…for centuries, people left home for San Francisco. And here I was.

"I think you'll love it here," he said. "I do. I really think it'll make you happy."

I wasn't so sure, but when Isaac said it, I believed him.

"Let's drop off your bags at my apartment," he said, "then we can go get some drinks."

It was nearly 5:00, but the air was still warm and the sun shone brightly. The streets were crowded with young people walking, but seemingly without a destination or worry. I was probably projecting, but I felt okay about that. I was excited to be in California, out west, to experience the antithesis of all I had ever known.

"This is it," he said, and we walked up the steps to a green apartment, two stories high, with white shutters. He unlocked the door then handed the key to me. "A spare," he said, "for you."

"Thank you," I said, still taking in my surroundings.

He led me up the stairs. "Would you like something to drink?

"A cup of water, please," I said, "and where is the restroom?"

"Right here," he said, jerking his left thumb over his shoulder, keeping his eyes on the glass he was filling. "Here," he set the full glass on a coaster on the table, "Let me put your bag in my bedroom."

I closed the door to the bathroom and took a moment before the mirror to collect myself. There was a time when Isaac meant everything to me. But I was a younger and more desperate person. I had put him on a pedestal. He turned out just to be another confused trans boy. My heart broke to pieces when our college affair never developed into anything more. I learned that he resented my moody devotion, calling it obsessive and needy to mutual acquaintances. He never included the fact that he encouraged it. He was fickle and difficult, but I knew I had made mistakes as well. We were young. We had forgiven each other. There was no reason to be so nervous around him now. He was just another person, just another trans guy, just a friend from long ago. We had been having really great long distance conversations- there was no reason I had to feel uncomfortable. Still, my hands shook as I turned on the sink and splashed some water on my face. I stroked the stubble on my chin with my thumb and forefinger. I looked into my own eyes. Yes, I felt handsome. I was ready. I flushed the toilet to keep up appearances, and let myself out.

Isaac sat at the table, leaning on his elbow and staring off into space. "Sit!" he said, nudging the adjacent chair with his foot, "You must be tired."

I sat beside him, sighing. "A little. But I'm always tired."

"Are you getting enough iron?"

"I…don't know," I said.

"Probably not," he said, "being a vegetarian and all."

I shrugged. There were several moments of silence. I took a sip of water. It was icy cold and it hurt my front teeth.

"So you lost your job," Isaac said.

I nodded, setting down my glass. "Yep."

"Did they give you any more of a reason?" he asked.

"No. I haven't talked to them or been to the library since," I said.

"But you think it was discrimination?"

I shrugged, sighing again and leaning back in my chair. "Well I'd have a hard time proving it. But given that they fired me a few days after someone put my book on hold…"

"Someone put it on hold? How do you know?"

52

"I saw it on the hold shelf. They ordered it from another library. I didn't even realize any libraries carried the thing."

"Neither did I." Isaac had started avoiding my eyes, I noticed. "That's impressive actually. But I mean, it's a great book so it makes sense."

"You really think so?"

"Of course. You're a fantastic writer...I've told you that so many times, why are you surprised?"

I smiled into my water glass, sipping again. It was true. I had sent *Refuse* his way before I'd published it, and I had received his approval and even some words of praise. Still, I always wondered what he really thought deep down.

"I mean obviously there were parts that were hard to read..." He said.

"I'm sorry," I said, cringing with guilt.

"No, it's fine. We've talked about this Elliott, I get it. It's fine. Do you want to go to bar? It's a little early, but people start early here."

"That's seriously all I want right now..."

"That's one of the things I love actually," he said. "There are just like queer dance parties in the middle of the day... I'll grab a bag. You'll want to bring a coat. It'll be cold when the sun goes down." He smiled. "You'll love this. It's always pea coat weather in San Francisco." Ah yes. He knew me well.

Isaac and I sat outside on the patio of the bar, sharing a joint. It was telling that no one gave us a second glance. A couple of other patrons were doing the same. The sun was bright and I felt comfortably warm and relaxed. I was glad I did this.

"What do you want to drink?" Isaac asked, after we had finished the joint.

"What ever you're having," I said, coughing.

He walked away from our table and up the steps to the door of the bar.

I leaned back in my chair and rested my knees against the table. There was a mural on the brick wall next to us that looked like a depiction of a Chiquita Banana drag queen. There were tall palm trees growing on either side and sporadically throughout the dirt patio area where we sat. Other trees as well, including a couple pines. I found the combination strangely hilarious and I started to laugh.

"Feeling good?" Isaac asked, returning and setting two pint glasses full of beer on our table. He rubbed my shoulder briefly and roughly, as he often used to. It was a gesture that always seemed somehow tongue-in-cheek yet affectionate. It was quintessentially him. Similarly, during the days when we were hooking up at Purchase, he would sometimes say, "Hey…buddy," and sort of shove me. He had this little awkward, slightly ironic look on his face that I never quite understood. "High five?" He would sometime add, making me glower, before he continued cuddling on the couch with Anna. I always did give him a high five though.

"This is a strange place," I said, lifting my beer to my lips. I took a sip. It was incredibly bitter. That's something I'm always surprised to appreciate, given my habit of going for Bud Light over craft beers. "Mm. What is this?"

"A local IPA," he said. "I can't remember what it's called. I just asked the bartender what he recommended."

"It's amazing," I said, taking a gulp.

"Take it slow," Isaac said. "It's stronger than most, and from what I recall, you're a bit of a lightweight."

I shrugged.

"How long do you plan on staying?" Isaac asked.

"How long will you have me?"

"Well, it's up to my roommates as well. But I'm sure a week is fine."

I nodded. "Cool."

"When's the book reading of yours?"

"Tomorrow at six," I said. "Do you want to come?"

"Of course!"

I smiled.

"So have you been doing with yourself?" Isaac asked. "Besides the library. Writing?"

"Yes," I said. "I've been working on a second book. I've been wanting to get an apartment with my friend Gabe, but now I'll probably have to keep living with my parents."

"Can't you find another job?"

"I suppose." The idea didn't thrill me. He sounded like my dad.

Isaac must have noticed my frown and he changed the subject. "So have you done many readings like this?"

"A few...I spoke at a community college in Syracuse, a university in Canada, a few other things. I'm still pretty new to this thing though."

"That's incredible though Elliott."

"Thank you."

"Really." He took another deep sip of his beer.

"Can I ask you something?" I said.

"Yes?"

"Do you still talk to Anna?"

"Yes," Isaac said. "I talked to her earlier today actually, on the phone."

"Ah," I said. "Does she still hate me?"

Isaac looked pensive. "It's not that she hates you," he said. "She's just hurt."

That was worse. "Maybe I should talk to her."

"Maybe," Isaac said. "I guess the main thing is, she feels you don't respect her. She can forgive what we did, and she can even forgive you writing about it. But she can't forgive your portrayal of her in the novel. It really hurt to see herself depicted that way...as this sort of clueless, ditsy femme girl."

I took my final sip of my drink—I always leave a little in the bottom. I can't have the last sip. It's a thing. "The irony is, when I wrote *Refuse,* I purposefully tried to make Maggie different. I thought it would be a betrayal of Anna to make the character too similar."

"I know," Isaac said, "But you have to look at it from her perspective."

"If I had based Maggie more on her, I would have made her funnier, brighter, queerer…with crazy hair and screaming about kitties and well, you know…I mean, Anna is larger than life. She would have made a great character. But my gut told me that was wrong. That's the sad part. I do respect her, and I don't really think she's anything like Maggie. Not that I even hate Maggie…but I guess she wasn't very three-dimensional. I was afraid to develop her as a character, and that was a failure on my part. I want to fix that."

Isaac nodded. "I mean I have to admit that I got upset reading some things in it. And yeah, I still worry see me as a pretty two dimensional person. Maybe that's my fault, I dunno. Maybe I present myself that way. And I have to admit, I hated the ending."

"I'm sorry," I said, "I don't see you that way. It wasn't supposed to be an accurate portrayal of you. It's hard to explain how fiction writing happens."

"No, I get it," Isaac said, "I really do. I'm just saying, I get where Anna's coming from too."

"Why did you hate the ending?" I asked. I lit another cigarette.

"I don't know," he said.

His eyes met mine and I was caught off guard. Was he saying he wished Colin and Dean ended up together? No, he couldn't be. He just didn't like it. Colin was an ass and that upset him.

"But I think you're a great writer," Isaac said. "And I think you're a really important voice. For trans people, I mean. What you're writing is very real, and unlike anything else out there. It's intense, but people need to hear it. I really appreciate it for that. It's raw."

I could tell he was getting drunk, because in the old days he would rarely praise me like this sober. That's one of the reasons I loved drinking with him in college. "God Elliott, you're so beautiful," he'd whisper to me in the kitchen where nobody could see us, stroking my arm. "I just want you all the time, I can't even handle it."

I'd close my eyes and soak it in, feeling the heat of his body against me, the damp sweat on his tee shirt, the masculine scent of him. It was as if I believed those words could cancel out all the verbal abuse I'd endured from others in my life—all those times I'd been told I was ugly, repulsive, awkward, worthless, just a girl...

"You're like a celebrity. With your perfect features, and your chiseled jaw line, and your perfect Morrissey hair. You're perfect."

Oh he could lay it on thick. He knew just how to charm the pants off me, and then somehow the precise wrong time to stop talking and cause the most heartache.

"I can't take my eyes off you. I can't help it, Elliott...I'm so gay. You're just everything I'm attracted to. You're sensitive and talented and gorgeous. It's not just when I'm drunk. I love you. I want you all the time..."

He was impossible—or at least highly improbable. Of course this was half a decade ago. But even then, what I wouldn't give to hear him say those words honestly, when sober, in perpetuity.

~~~

Isaac came with me to my book reading. As mentioned, I was published in a transgender anthology released earlier that year. The anthology was nominated for the Lambda Literary Awards. There were several new categories this year, including Transgender Fiction. Rarely, if ever, did you see fiction written about transgender people and by transgender people. Now it was becoming a thing, coincidentally at the same time I self-published my first book. So does it mean fiction written by transgender people? About transgender people? For transgender people? My short answer is, I don't know. But evidently I'm writing it, and I'm probably stuck with it, for better and for worst.

The reading was at the San Francisco Public Library, downtown. We followed signs down to the basement. On a pillar there was a flyer for the event. I noticed my picture among several other writers, with my name beneath, spelled "Elliot." I nudged Isaac. "Look at that."

"You're famous!" he said.

I smiled. "Hardly. Do you think it's in there?" I asked, nodding towards the double doors to our right.

"Probably," he said.

I stayed planted. After a few seconds, I said, "I'm actually really nervous to go in."

"You'll be great," he said.

I took a deep breath and followed a group of people inside.

I scanned the room, looking for anyone I recognized. Everyone looked older than me. Lots of other white people – gay men and lesbians, I presumed. They were hanging around the snack table and drinking out of paper cups. Isaac and I stood there, lost, until I saw my author friend Tonya, in the second row of chairs, waving.

"Hello!" We both said as she rose to her feet to hug me. I'd actually only met Tonya one other time in person, when she had come to speak at Syracuse University. I loved her performance of her work, and I bought a copy of her book, which I also loved. She was an older transgender woman of color, and most of her essays and poems I had read were related to her identity. She was easy to connect with, and we'd talked a fair amount online since then. Perhaps to call her my friend was a stretch, but I felt like I knew her from reading her work. I introduced her and Isaac to one another, and then we sat.

After a sufficient amount of small talk, I said, "Tonya…if you were a young trans writer…Well, if you were me, and you were trying to make it as a writer, where would you live?"

She thought about this, furrowing her brow. "New York," she said, definitively.

That's what I'd expected, and not really what I wanted to hear. I had big, complicated feelings about New York City.

Several people read excerpts from their work, some of which grabbed me and some of which didn't. It was kind of like a game of duck-duck-goose. Gay. Lesbian. Gay. Lesbian. Gay. Lesbian. Transgender! There were three of us: Tonya, me, and a second gay-looking trans guy named Cal. His picture had also been on the flyer outside. He did porn. He also had a short story in the same anthology.

Of the three trans writers, Tonya read first. Her story was about a number of things, mainly backpacking through Europe with her girlfriend. I looked around the room, wondering how many people knew she was trans before it was announced she was nominated for "Best Transgender Nonfiction." How many of the women in the room were still threatened by transgender women infiltrating their lesbian communities? With her kind voice and friendly demeanor, how could anyone see Tonya as a threat? Perhaps I wasn't giving these folks enough credit.

Gay. Lesbian. Gay. Elliott! I was up. I hadn't decided exactly which part of the story I was going to read until I reached the podium. Clearing my throat, I leaned towards the microphone. I explained that this was also an excerpt of my novel *Refuse*, which I was on the back table with the other books for sale if anyone was interested.

I read a scene in which Dean and Teddy, a trans man and a trans woman, respectively, are standing outside after a transgender support group.

"I don't know why I even bother," Teddy said, *"those men think I'm a crazy-cat lady before I even open my mouth...and don't think it's just a guy thing...They think I don't know I look like a guy in a wig?"* She continues on, explaining how the other trans women in her town have labeled her a "fetishist" and not a "real trans woman." Dean listens quietly as she expresses her frustration with the hypocrisy of a trans community that expects her to fit a mold. "I wasn't meant to blend in. If I wanted to, I wouldn't have transitioned in the first place."

Dean responds, *"Oscar Wilde said that when the gods wish to punish us, they answer our prayers."*

"That fat pedophile had an answer for everything, didn't he?"

Several audience members laughed. Maybe too hard, actually. Perhaps the crowd was to eager break the tension. An encounter with even a *literary* form of transgender rage was perhaps too much for the evening. Teddy would probably find little acceptance either among the demographic represented tonight.

"It was great," Isaac whispered to me when I returned to my seat. "You could tell it made people really uncomfortable…in the best way."

"You think so?"

"Definitely."

"I worried I seemed to shy and awkward."

"But that's your thing. That's what people like about you. You're authentic."

Several other people read, including the other trans guy who was about ten times more confident and loud than me.

After the reading was done, Isaac left to find a restroom. I remained in the room in a half-hearted attempt to mingle. Turning towards the table of now dried-out cheese and grapes, I found my path blocked by a tall man I'd estimate was in his late forties.

Guy: You're from Syracuse?

Me: Yes.

Guy: I hate that place.

Me: Ha, oh...?

Guy: Why Syracuse?

Me: What?

Guy: Did you grow up there or something?

Me: Yeah.

Guy: I lived there for two years when I was in college back in the 90s. It sucks. Though there were pretty buildings, like Victorian or something.

Me: Yeah definitely.

Guy: I know a guy around here who's from Syracuse. Really miserable guy. Really self-hating. All the gay guys there were like that.

Me: Ha!

Guy: They weren't even gay in the sense that we're gay here. They were like Neanderthal gays...not to say that you are like that.

Me: No, I would say that's an accurate description, sadly.

Guy: Make sure you get out of there!

Me: Mm.

It struck me as rather presumptuous. As far as I'm concerned, someone's hometown is like family – even if they talk shit about it, you should refrain. I gave up on socializing with the queer literati and went out into the hall to find Isaac. I was ready to get some drinks and complain about shit, just the two of us.

"You'll never believe what just happened," I said, smirking as I approached.

"Funny, I was going to say the same thing to you."

"You first."

He told me how he overheard a pair of older women, presumably lesbians, talking outside in the hall.

"So there sure are a lot of transgendered writers this year," one said.

There were 3 out of the 18 writers in attendance, for the record. I wouldn't call that a lot.

"How do you feel about it?" She asked.

"I don't like it," the other woman said.

"Me neither."

"Welcome to San Francisco," I muttered darkly.

~~~

Friday night. I had a gin and tonic, two beers, and two shots of tequila. Still, I felt awkward and miserable. I wasn't even sure where I was. I knew it was Oakland, and I knew there was a bar and a dance floor, but that's about it. Oh, and it was a queer dance party called Ships in the Night. It apparently moved around and was hosted at a different place each time. While waiting in line, I was already high, and I waxed-poetic about that name.

"Ships in the Night. How sad."

Isaac shrugged. "I think it's kind of like…you know, romanticizing the culture where queers hook up and then go their own separate ways. Like, *live for tonight,* you know?"

"I know. But that's sad to me."

I went out to smoke on the patio. It was so, so crowded inside. I could barely squeeze past the anonymous, sweating bodies, glowing red under the lights. I managed it though, and I found a place to sit on a bench off to the left. Many people were outside as well. I lit my cigarette and took a drag. Looking up, I could see the night sky. Again, a palm tree was silhouetted, but it was hardly paradise. It was gritty and urban, and I appreciated it for that. Yet I couldn't quite pinpoint why I was so unhappy. It was good writing research, if nothing else. Why was I insistent on moping?

Isaac had disappeared almost as soon as we arrived. I told him it was fine. I mean, I didn't want him hanging out with me if he didn't want to. He kept telling me again and again that this was also a vacation for him, because he barely ever took time off work. I didn't want to hold him back. He wasn't obligated to hang out with me the entire week.

The previous night we'd even gone our separate ways. He wanted to go out for drinks with work friends and I just wasn't in the mood to meet new people. It had been nice for a while. I walked around on my own, listening to my music, poking my head in a few cafés and bookstores. I was used to my silent, suburban walks. In my neighborhood, the streets were vacant before the sun even set. That was the time I felt most comfortable venturing out into the world. Here the streets were bustling with life, at least on the main roads like Mission and Valencia, which is where I had ended up. It was a little overwhelming at the time, and not something to which I thought I could ever grow accustomed.

That night, I discovered an excellent thrift store called Out of the Closet. I was rifling through jeans when a man came up next to me. He was a little older and bigger than me, not bad looking, with a flat cap and a navy track jacket. He started looking through the jeans as well. "As if I need any more clothes," he said in an effeminate drawl, giving me a look that seemed to say *you know how it is.* I was caught of guard, so I only smiled and nodded. Later, I watched as he and a second man waited in line at the register. His friend looked Latino, with thick black hair styled similar to my own quiff, and a thin chinstrap beard. They touched a lot, in a way that suggested intimacy but was in no way showy or gushy: a light, teasing shove, fixing the other's hair, gently leaning against each other... I realized the man probably wasn't talking about clothes but rather acknowledging me as one of them—maybe even flirting, harmlessly.

They moved confidently, as if this was their space, as if they had just as much a right to this spot of ground as anyone else—as if they didn't even give it a second thought. Outside, through the window, I saw them kiss. My chest ached. In many ways, it was easier when you didn't see it: when no queer was happy and it was therefore Syracuse, not me, that was to blame.

I texted Isaac.

There was actually little elbowroom at all. I wasn't sure if it was a gay bar—most San Francisco bars seemed gayer than the ones to which I was accustomed. It was small, dark, loud, and packed. I looked around, trying to appear nonchalant, my heart pounding with nerves. I still hadn't got a hold on my social anxiety, despite what I tried to tell myself. I spotted Isaac. He was seated at a booth in the back with about five others. He waved and I hurried over to him. I barely saw anyone as he introduced me—a boy with a beard, another boy might have worn a hat, and there were several others I can't remember. A girl—brown hair, that's all I recall—was seated very close to Isaac on his right. I suspected she was the one he mentioned earlier. They'd made out or something and he'd liked her at one point.

I excused myself to the bathroom. It was a tiny room with one stall. A man was using the urinal, or at least trying to. I realized I didn't actually need to go to the bathroom, so I left. Back in the bar, I glanced Isaac's way. He was talking to the girl and didn't see me. I decided just to leave. I didn't want to go to that place in my head.

I sat on a bench by a tree, crossing my legs and smoking a cigarette. I wondered where Isaac had wandered. I didn't want to be a ship in the night on my own. He was probably on the dance floor, because he enjoyed that kind of thing, at least when drunk—that was why we had come in the first place. I texted him.

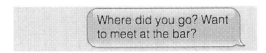

Where did you go? Want to meet at the bar?

He met me at a little table in the corner about five minutes later. His red-blonde hair was swept off his forehead. His cheeks were flushed. He was always self-conscious about his sweating but I didn't think it was that bad. Those are all signs that someone is moving and alive, that there blood is circulating. My hands and feet were always cold and my head faint. That's much less attractive.

"Having a good time?" I asked.

He nodded. "You're not." It wasn't a question.

"Sorry," I mumbled. "It's just not my kind of thing. Not tonight, at least."

He nodded again, looking around. "We should go soon anyway. The last train back to San Francisco leaves at midnight."

I followed him down a hall. It had dark wood walls and was poorly lit. I wondered what kind of building this was. It didn't seem like a normal bar. I followed him up a carpeted staircase to a second floor I hadn't known existed. There were more benches and tables, but less people. Two boys were making out in the corner and three girls were seated on a couch, staring off into space. I leaned on the ledge, looking down on the dance floor below. So many people—different shapes, sizes, races, genders—were dancing furiously, all aglow under the red light. The music was loud, thumping in my chest. I caught a few words. *We fell in love in a hopeless place. We fell in love in a hope-less place.*

I wondered if I had misheard. It seemed like something I would make up. I *was* falling in love, wasn't I? Or maybe I never crawled out of love in the first place. But where was the hopeless place? It couldn't be San Francisco, which seemed to me the quintessence of queer promise and possibilities. Syracuse was the obvious answer—little dreary old Syracuse. But I hadn't found love there. I didn't think I ever would. That was the problem. That's partially why I was there.

Perhaps the song hadn't meant a physical place, but a shared emotional state. That was the only way I could make sense of it in my confused and drunk stupor—the kind that made me believe the universe centered on my melodramas.

Some women were on the stage now, talking about how important our health is—*especially trans folk, who are so lacking in resources.* They were representing an LGBT clinic, I believe. Acceptance this, love that, *everybody deserves healthcare even if they can't pay...we all deserve happiness and health and love!* At least that's what I heard. Who knows.

I started to cry. Not about the evening, but about my entire life—the years upon years wasted hating myself and hiding in North Syracuse, not going to the doctor when I was sick, avoiding the neighbors. Night upon night wishing I would die in my sleep, not wanting to wake again to the lonely, painful, meaningless daily routine. I cried over the hatred I had endured from people's parents, classmates, employers, strangers—the taunts, the threats, the secrets I kept—the weight of abuse, the dehumanization—medically, sexually, self-critically—that heavy hatred of my very skin, my very physical form. For at least a decade I had nothing but disgust and detachment from my body, which in reality was all I ever had, and all I would ever get. And above all else, I was so, so tired of being alone. *That's what gets you in the end. The loneliness.* What was that from?

Isaac came to stand beside me. He saw me crying, despite my attempts to hide it. "Do you need a hug?" he asked, sheepish, the whites of his eyes red with intoxication and the effects of medical marijuana.

I nodded, feeling an ache in my limbs that seemed to underscore my timid longing. I put my arms around his neck and he circled his around my waist. His upper body was much broader than my own and I loved the way he felt—the way our flat, scarred chests pressed together through our tee shirts, the way his hands felt as they rubbed my back, the way he gave me a tight squeeze of reassurance. I sobbed into his shoulder until he pulled away.

Twenty minutes later we were in the streets of Oakland. Isaac was stressed, as he always was, but now especially. He had lost his green track jacket and was afraid we would miss the last train back to San Francisco.

"It's fine," I said, drunkenly stumbling over the curb as the white "walk" sign lit up in the dark. "Everything is great."

"No," he said. "We've got to hurry. We're going to miss it and we'll be stranded."

"Relax," I said, "Is a beautiful night. Jus' slow down. We can always stay..." I panted a bit, "... in a hotel. S'okay."

Isaac shook his head, staring down at the map on his cell phone.

"Gimme a sec," I said, bending over with my hands on my knees. I'd heard once that if you put your head between your legs, it helped with nausea. I really didn't want to puke in the street like I did my first night in Brooklyn. Isaac had been there that night as well. I heaved several heavy breaths, in through my nose and out through my mouth. When I looked up, Isaac was running away from me, already pretty far in the distance.

"Isaac!" I shouted. "Hey! Wait..." He turned around the corner. By the time I managed to get there myself, he was nowhere in sight.

I called him several times on my cell but got no response.

I texted,

Come back...

...and then said it aloud, pitifully. I slumped down against the stone building onto the grimy sidewalk. I could feel vertigo edging in. "Remember this when you're sober," I thought. "This is Isaac, just as much as the guy who hugs you and understands. This is him as well. He has no trouble abandoning you." I closed my eyes. I wondered if Isaac was right that people out here can recognize a trans guy from a cis guy, even on T. I wondered whether it was legal to sleep on a sidewalk if there was no sign telling you not to.

My phone lit up in my limp hand and vibrated. It was Isaac.

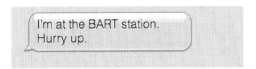
I'm at the BART station.
Hurry up.

I took a deep breath and pocketed my phone. I sprung to my feet, surprising myself, and took off running as fast as I could. I couldn't feel my legs, so it seemed like I was flying, or at least riding a bike. The air was cold. Isaac had my cardigan in his bag.

Miraculously, I found the station. I guess we weren't far. Isaac was standing at the bottom of the stairs.

"You left me," I said.

"I thought you would follow me," he said, staring straight ahead.

"Oh."

The train arrived seconds later with a heavy gust. The car was mostly empty. We found two seats together in the back.

"I'm sorry about your jacket," I said, again.

"It's fine," he said.

I knew it wasn't. I knew that little things took on big meanings when he was drunk and disappointed. Looking at him, you would think the entire queer San Francisco community had just betrayed him.

"Maybe somebody was drunk and took it by accident," I said.

"Honestly," he said, "it's easier for me to just figure someone stole it and be angry. Otherwise I feel like an idiot."

"Oh," I said. "Well, you shouldn't..." Full of liquid courage, I reached out and took his hand. He let me. He even rubbed mine a little with his thumb. A moment later, I was hit with nausea and doubled over. I rested my head on his knee, and when he stroked my hair, I decided just to lay across his lap. He continued running his fingers through my hair and rubbing my back.

"Don't worry," I said, "I'm not gonna throw up."

Perhaps triggered by my words, the boy in the seat in front of us started to vomit violently. He was thin, somewhat delicate, and alone. After wiping his mouth on his sleeve, he started to cry. I sat up, wincing, and leaned forward.

"It's OK, friend," I said, rubbing the strange boy's shoulder. "It's OK. We're in this together."

Mustang convertibles were half off at the rental agency. Isaac was a little hesitant because he thought he would look ridiculous driving it, but I could tell he really wanted to do it. I'd never been in a convertible before.

We got a white one and headed for the coast. We kept the top up while we were still in the city. I'd spent the past few days walking around on my own while Isaac was working. How different San Francisco seemed from a car! I felt like we owned the city, as opposed to my usual feeling that I was out of place. I felt wealthy and mature and free. Isaac just kept grinning, making me grin as well. We listened to music with an auxilary cord hooked up to our phones. First we were listening to Morrissey, because he isn't that familiar with his solo work and said he wanted to be and I nearly died of happiness, putting on *Bona Drag* to begin. But then we got talking about Nico and so he wanted me to listen to *Chelsea Girls* because I'd never really gotten into that album and he thought I'd like it. I did, but it wasn't suiting my mood. Speaking of albums I couldn't get into— Joni Mitchell's *Blue*. Oh, that couldn't stand—Isaac had to put it on immediately. "It's so perfect," he had said. "It's so California. Joni is an emo songstress you need to love."

"It's a good thing we have hours left of driving," I said. There was so much to listen to still, and no way we'd ever get through it all.

The clouds started to clear as we reached Highway One. There were beautiful green hills on both sides of the winding road. We put up the top, and the sensation was like nothing I'd ever experienced before. I kept turning my head, in awe of the panorama forming before my eyes. The breeze blew through my hair. Maybe it was just the atmosphere but seriously, I couldn't comprehend how I ever disliked this album. This woman had the voice of a goddamn angel. And the words...

I am on a lonely road and I am traveling

Looking for something, what can it be?

Oh I hate you some, I hate you some, I love you some

Oh I love you when I forget about me.

I wanna be strong, I wanna laugh along

I wanna belong to the living...

I looked at Isaac and I nearly cried. I can't remember ever seeing him genuinely happy. I'm sure I had, but I don't remember it, and that said something. So often, his smiles were tired and sad. "I needed this," he said. When he turned back to the road, I took his picture. And it occurred to me that I usually would want a picture of myself in such a situation, because I'm awful and conceited like that. But I wasn't thinking about me for once. *I love you when I forget about me.* It was liberating, just like Joni Mitchell made it sound. But a part of me couldn't help thinking maybe it wasn't the best idea to get too caught up in the moment. It usually didn't end well when I forgot about me.

And then I saw the ocean around the bend. "Isaac, look!"

Was this really America? Could this really be our home? I mean sure, New York State's got its share of natural beauty. But this? This had to be another country.

~~~

We stopped at a state park in Big Sur. My aunt told me there was a waterfall here that poured into the ocean: Julia Pfiefer Falls. Isaac was still driving. We had agreed that was best, because other people's driving caused him great anxiety, and I similarly recognized that criticism of my driving sent me through the roof, recalling the time I had practically screamed at Gabe's boyfriend for making snarky remarks in the back seat.

Isaac and I both knew that our friendship was a strange one. A congenial pair, rarely did we argue face-to-face. And yet something explosive lurked beneath the surface, for better and for worst. With my luck, all my romantic longing, sexual tension, and lingering resentment for our college years would come spilling out in a bellow of, "I CAN JUST TURN THIS CAR AROUND AND YOU CAN WALK HOME." Which, of course, he couldn't. I was therefore proud of us for being so mature as to recognize our own weaknesses, and I thought it bade well for our future as a... Wait—I was thinking of us as a couple, wasn't I? Shit. When had the change taken place in my mind? When did I switch over? I glanced at him as we drove through a thicket of massive pines. He looked extraordinarily serious focused on the road. It made me smirk. Fuck. I really liked him.

We reached a kiosk. It looked empty.

"Do we have to pay?" Isaac asked, slowly creeping past in the Mustang. I shrugged.

A woman emerged from the darkness of the kiosk. "Um, excuse me? You have to pay." Her tone was hostile and condescending. As Isaac apologized, I fixed her with a glare. *Don't talk to him like that,* I thought. And perhaps I'd just spent too long in Syracuse, but I was quite convinced she'd marked us as faggots and hated us for it. I wasn't naive enough to think everyone in the San Francisco Bay area was open-minded. I imagined there were hordes of them who wanted to take their land back from our homosexual clutches, and she was undoubtedly one of them. Or she might have just been having a bad day.

"It's ten dollars," she said.

"*Okay*," I said, with obvious sass. "I don't have cash," I said to Isaac.

"I don't either. We'll have to drive to an ATM. There was one at the convenience store."

We looped around and parked off to the side and out of sight. "I wanna smoke first," Isaac said, turning off the ignition.

"That's so stupid," I said, "making us pay to see nature! How can they say they *own* a waterfall? I fucking hate that." Isaac was lighting his pipe. When he finished, he handed it to me.

I easily slip into righteous, indignant rant mode. I would have kept going on about capitalism and the state and mother earth if I hadn't noticed his face. "Hey are you alright?"

Isaac was staring at the steering wheel and gripping his hair with both hands.

"Isaac?"

"Yeah," he said. "It'll be fine. I just need to take a deep breath."

"What's the matter?"

"I just get stressed," he said. "The weed helps, but it takes a little while to kick in."

"Why are you stressed?" I asked. "Because of that woman? Don't be!" I passed him back the bowl and he lit up once more.

"I just get feeling pressured when people visit me," he said. "Like I've got to make sure you don't have a bad time..."

I hadn't any idea about this and probably looked somewhat bewildered. "What? I'm having a great time!" I said. "Can't you tell? Besides, it wouldn't be your fault if I wasn't."

"I just like to have a schedule," he said. "And I hate when things go wrong. I get stressed."

"But who cares? We don't even have to go, really."

"Nooo." Then, realizing he was being somewhat ridiculous, he said in a heavy-metal voice, "We're eating our lunch under a waterfall...and it's going to be magical!"

We both laughed.

"Look," I said, "what's the worst that could happen?"

"We go off to find an ATM and I get us lost in the middle of nowhere."

"So...?"

"And our phones die so we can't figure out how to get home."

"So...we rent a cheap motel. It'd be fun."

"But you wouldn't get to see the things you wanted to see."

"We could check them out tomorrow instead," I said, "and so what? I'll be back, trust me. This place is amazing. I'm having an amazing time. Really."

He nodded and started up the car. "Yeah," he said, "me too." He sounded less than certain.

"Oh wait," I said, looking inside my wallet again and laughing. "I think totally had ten dollars the whole time."

He took a deep breath and winced. "If you do, just...don't tell me. It's fixed. We worked it out. I don't want to know." I cocked my head in confusion like a bird. I don't know why, but I almost had the nerve to kiss him again. I didn't though.

Back at the kiosk, we discovered we were actually at the wrong park. So, once again, we looped around and headed back out on the highway. I tried to glance at Isaac now and again without being obvious. Why had our relationship always been so complicated? He seemed to me, at this moment, a complete mystery. I could accept that I had gotten him wrong, but it still was scary to consider that I still loved him. I shoved the thought away, focusing instead on the amazing seascape to my right and the unfamiliar music coming through the stereo.

We were somewhat disappointed when we realized we couldn't go down to the beach to get close to the waterfall. Rather, we could walk along a dirt path weaving along the cliffs and look at it from above as it poured into the ocean. It was so beautiful that I couldn't stay sad for long.

We were drunk and high, with only a rope fence between us and death. As usual, I couldn't shut up.

"I pretended to be Harry Potter most everyday," I told him. "And I got depressed when I had to stop. It was so *trans* in retrospect. From age three or so, I was always pretending to be some fictional male character. I'd say up until as old as fourteen. And when I didn't find it fulfilling anymore, I panicked, because I didn't know who I was."

Isaac was walking beside me, eying a group of straight, loud Asian boys with suspicion as they walked towards us. He waited until we had passed them to speak. "I understand that," he said. "I played with Legos until that age. I went from being obsessed with Legos to obsessed with sex."

I laughed. "I never had the patience for Legos. I was either pretending to be someone or I was enacting some sort of intense story between my animal toys—oh the interpersonal drama of Beanie Babies...you have no idea. But no, no Legos or Tinker Toys or any of that crap. That was for my brother. I hated building things. I did sometimes pretend Lincoln Logs were cigars..."

"I liked it," he said, "But it was more than that. There was a whole universe I invented...it was, well, a Robin Hood universe."

"Robin Hood?"

"Yes. I'll tell you more about it some time when I'm a little less stoned. Right now I've got to rest."

We stopped to catch our breath. The sun was starting to set. I looked out at rocks that were perched in the ocean. I stared far off into the dark water, wondering what kinds of marine animals dwelled below the surface.

"Strangely," Isaac said, "you and I sort of fit the typical trans narrative, don't we? More so than anyone else I've known. I've always felt a little embarrassed about that."

"In the abstract, yes," I said. "The major details are pretty typical. I mean I've got all these super-sad-little-trans-kid stories. For instance, the day my neighbor told me I wasn't allowed in her pool unless I put on a girl swimsuit and covered my chest. Already at age four, I felt this deep sense of shame and disgust with myself."

"When I was that age, I pretended to be Aladdin," he said. "I wore this little open vest and drew hair on my chest and face with a Magic Marker."

I laughed aloud. "Aladdin totally didn't have a beard or chest hair..."

"I know," Isaac said, smiling, "that's what makes it so trans." His eyes were such a lovely shade of blue, like the water below. There were a million other stories like this—some of them I'd heard but would listen to again and again if he wanted to tell me. My affection for him was seemingly boundless.

"In a way," I said, "not to discredit our other friends or people I've known...but you're the only other like, full-on, text-book, transsexual male I've ever been close to. Or at least, the only other guy who's gone through surgery, a name change, the whole ordeal, just like me. It's more than our identities at this point – it's our bodies too. They don't fit. Usually, I feel alone in that. Do you get what I mean?"

"I feel almost guilty about it," he said. "Being so...typical."

"I know," I said, "it's strange. I forget that it's hard for me, until I see you. I tell myself I pass as a middle-class white man now: I don't feel I have a right to be hurting. But when I talk with you, it all comes to the fore, and I'm reminded of all those invisible burdens and secrets and, well, *traumas*. Not in a way that we sit around feeling sorry for ourselves...I mean, when we're together we're usually laughing. It's just...I don't know. It's really validating to be with you."

But Isaac had severed the connection. Something about his body language shut it down, and his lack of response was chilling, causing an achy lump in the back of my throat. Not for the first time, I was aware there were things in his past that he hadn't told me—things that

78

couldn't be laughed off like our masculine childhood yearnings. Big things. Painful things. Or who knows. Maybe he was just stressed about the time. Maybe he sensed my feelings and didn't reciprocate them. That seemed most likely. I bit my lip and looked off at the waterfall, committing it to memory.

~~~

After we left Big Sur, we decided to stay the night in Santa Cruz. We split the cost of a motel room at an America's Best. Isaac parked the car, feeling a little nervous it might get jacked, and we spent a good ten minutes trying to locate the front desk. Eventually we found a woman behind a kiosk who told us sixty a night for a two-bedroom.

"How much for one-bedroom?" Isaac asked.

"One-bedroom?" she said in a Mexican accent, raising an eyebrow and giving us a look over. "Fifty."

"We'll take that," Isaac said firmly. "You know, to save money." My insides squirmed with joy.

She gave us another skeptical look then jotted something down and handed him the keys, saying nothing more to us.

"Wow," I whispered.

"I feel like she thinks we're little boys running away from home," Isaac said, frowning.

"No way," I said. 'Isaac, you have a beard…and I basically do too at this point," I said, eyeing my unshaved face in the window reflection. "She's just homophobic."

We looked all over for room thirty but couldn't find it. There was an arrow for rooms thirty to fifty, but it appeared to lead to the road.

"Oh my god," I said, "I bet that there *is* no room thirty. I bet that's what they tell people they don't want staying there! Then they see the arrow, leading to the road, which means *Hit the road, faggots!"*

"No Elliott," Isaac said, "You're just really high." Sure enough, he was right. I can't remember how, but we found the room. It was very small but clean and tidy enough. The bed was twin-sized and unpleasantly firm. After skimming through all the cable TV channels, we decided to go back out for a drive to check out the beach.

We couldn't tell if the boardwalk was open. We parked down by the arcade games. Everything was dark, but the sign said open and the gates weren't locked. Some of the games were lit up, and there was one of those creepy mechanical fortune-tellers. I really wanted my fortune told, but we kept moving. I love that sort of thing. It gives me the creeps in the best way possible. I would have loved to take Isaac's hand as we passed the dim, twinkling carnival lights and the eerie carnival organ music. We were the only ones on the beach, so we sat down and opened some more beers Isaac was stowing in his backpack. I don't know what we laid on. I don't think we had a blanket, so we probably just sat in the sand.

"The best explanation I've heard for anxiety," I said, "is that we are animals, and we go into fight-or-flight mode when attacked. Our instincts kick in. If enough times in our life we've had to deal with serious stressors and attacks, we lose our ability to monitor our reaction. Pretty soon, everything sets us off. Like a hair-trigger response."

"That's very accurate," Isaac said.

It meant a lot to be trusted like this, even if the alcohol and drugs played a factor. I had very few people I considered close friends. My anxious instinct told me to cling tightly; Isaac's told him to run. I fought; Isaac took flight.

Back at the room, we watched TV – some late night show or other. Lying beside him, my heart raced, and I dared myself again and again to do something, anything. I don't know how he would have reacted. Eventually, I gave up on action – I decided I had to say something instead. This proved equally difficult, as my mouth seemed incapable of forming the sounds. I lay on my side with my head awkwardly close to his arm. He was on his back. In retrospect, I must have been obvious. My face was undoubtedly scrunched up in thought as I slowly inched closer. Finally, I was able to make a sound. "Um…"

He looked down at me.

"I…" my throat was dry but I pushed myself to say it. I only had a couple days left with him. If not now, when? "I really want…to be physical with you," I said. I immediately hid my face in the pillow afterwards, turning red.

Several seconds passed. I turned my head slightly to look up at him.

"I mean...we can cuddle?" he said, opening his arms up, half-apologetically. "I don't know...?"

"OK," I said, "Are you sure you want to?"

"Yeah," he said.

His tone was believable enough for me. I edged over and nestled into the space between his shoulder and hips so that he could wrap his right arm around my back. I rested my head on his chest and, unsure what to do with my right arm, I cautiously draped it across his upper ribcage. I felt my body warm pleasantly with that adolescent sensation once more. I was struck by the girth of his upper body in comparison to my own – beyond his being heavier than me, we had vital differences in our bone structures. I know there are large, broad women in this world, and I know that testosterone injections have many masculinizing effects on the body. But as I unclenched my fist and gently grazed my fingers over his tee shirt and chest, my arm reaching across and resting upon his torso, I felt certain that he was biologically male – that something in his makeup had predetermined his transsexuality. I couldn't picture him as a woman. It was more than just the feel of his body – it was his energy. Touching him felt like truly knowing him, beyond our words. I was welcomed back to his body, and I recognized the familiar pull, like there was a magnet in my chest. My brain quieted, and if I had any coherent inner dialogue, it was simply one-word thoughts– Yes. Happiness. Love. Home.

He caressed my bare shoulder as I moved my hand back and forth across his chest. I moved slowly, in order that he could yell "Stop!" at any time, and I could perhaps deny having done anything sensual in the first place.

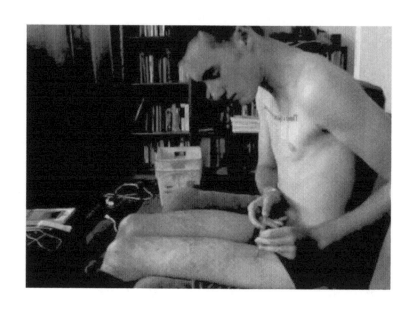

Part Three

I moved from Syracuse to Santa Cruz in July. It was chilly in the mornings, and I huddled up with a blanket and a mug of coffee in the breakfast nook. One of my first nights at my new place, I walked to the ocean. Though it was too cloudy to see the sky, I stayed on Seabright Beach until the sun went down and it was dusk. There were several sailboats out on the water, bobbing about and moving with the breezes. The waves rolled in, and I walked along the shore with my shoes off and my jeans rolled up to my knees. To my left was a lighthouse. The wharf to my right, the location of The Boardwalk, "the world's best seaside amusement park."

I hadn't found work, so I mostly spent my days walking the streets without a destination in mind, talking to cats on the sidewalk and getting sun-burnt. I knew I couldn't afford this lifestyle for long. I only had a couple thousand in savings, but I was really making it count. I still drank a lot of champagne, which I found to be a very gentle-drunk experience. Sometimes I couldn't even tell I was intoxicated until I tried to talk to one of my housemates or found myself falling asleep at the keyboard.

I walked to the beach often. One day I even swam. It was the mid afternoon and it was very crowded. I was wearing my little green trunks that end at my mid thighs. I hadn't seen any other men who wear shorts this short – only in New York, and maybe San Francisco. As I walked down Seabright Ave, I felt the eyes of pedestrians and drivers. I was also wearing mid-calf blue tube socks with white stripes, like a seventies's gay porn star. At one point, someone yelled something at me from a car. I couldn't understand the words, but it was said in a fake lisp.

At the beach, I had to be the only person older than ten with my feet in the water. The children and I would inch a little deeper, before the waves came roaring and we'd run grinning and giggling for the shore. My shorts were noticeably effeminate when surrounded by boys and men with trunks that sagged beneath their knees. I didn't care. I didn't even care that when the fabric was wet and clinging to the smooth curve of my crotch. I liked it. I knew I was sexy in my strange way, and if others denied it, that was only because it made them uncomfortable or they didn't understand it. Besides, I wasn't out to impress anybody – just splash around and laugh like a little child. It was a new feeling, and I revelled in it.

The water wasn't as cold as I anticipated. I did a shallow swan dive, feeling the wonderful coolness surround my body, then came up to breathe and wipe the salt from my eyes. After repeating this several times, riding the waves on my stomach, nearly knocking down a group of girls, I returned to my towel and just lay in the bright light for a half hour or so, trying my best to keep the grin on my face and the continued rejection by Isaac out of my mind.

People I met would inevitably asked, "What brings you here?" I gave the most honest answer possible: "I'm not sure. I just really needed to get away."

From a conservative suburb of dreary rustbelt city to a liberal tourist town on the ocean, full of hippies, students, and surfers– you could almost see them as caricatures of the East and West. Syracuse, miserable. Santa Cruz, out of touch. It was hard to know who I was when taken out of context. I found the experience utterly disorienting, and perhaps that, coupled with the champagne, was why I sometimes found myself wishing I was a girl.

The seaside amusement park's neon colors glowed in the distance and there were sounds of screaming from the roller coasters. The sun had set only a few hours earlier. I went there almost every night by bicycle, to sit alone on the beach, listen to the dark waves and stargaze. To be truthful, most the time I was listening to my headphones, and I only heard the ocean between tracks. My playlist included:

1. Fleetwood Mac's Greatest Hits (the Stevie Nicks' ones): Gypsy, Storms, Dreams, Rhiannon, Sara, Landslide, Silver Spring

2. Joni Mitchell's Blue: All I Want, Carey, A Case of You, This Flight Tonight, California

3. Joni Mitchell's Don Juan's Reckless Daughter: Talk to Me, Jericho, the title track

4. Other Joni Mitchell: Both Sides Now, I Don't Know Where I Stand, Don't Interrupt the Sorrow, The Same Situation

5. Morrissey: Jack the Ripper, Let Me Kiss You, I Am Two People, I'd Love To, Wide To Receive, Billy Budd, I Am Hated for Loving, Sunny, My Dearest Love,

6. Rufus Wainwright: Grey Gardens, Going to a Town, Go or Go Ahead, Pretty Things

7. The National: Bloodbuzz Ohio, I'm Afraid of Everyone, Graceless, The Geese of Beverly Road, I Should Live in Salt, Anyone's Ghost

8. Dione Warwick: I'll Never Fall in Love Again, Loneliness Remembers What Happiness Forgets, Knowing When to Leave, Raindrops Keep Falling on My Head

9. Aretha Franklin: Share Your Love With Me

10. Nina Simone: Love Me or Leave Me

11. R.E.M.: The One I Love

12. Mazzy Star: Fade Into You

13. Neko Case: Night Still Comes

Well you get the idea. It was a strange, repetitive, dramatic mix that fueled my walks and the fire of my despair. Yet somehow it helped too, as I found myself morphing into the vocalists, if only for a few minutes, and feeling their mysterious parallel pain instead of my own.

LittleKing was the username of the guy I was meeting. Why was I meeting him? Good question. Probably because I was so sad that I couldn't stand it. Other times when I felt this way, I would go in the bathroom with tweezers and pull out my body hairs for nearly an hour. I can't explain why.

I wasn't just sad that Isaac seemed increasingly uninterested in me. I had barely heard from him since moving out here. He took days to respond to texts. He showed reluctance to see me at all. But I was sad long before I had gotten my hopes up for him. I had gotten to the point where I didn't even ask why anymore. It was just a fact of existence. Living was sad- I was mature enough to recognize this now and not do anything too hasty, beyond my bizarre and secretive compulsions.

Earlier that day, my housemate Lucas and I had gone to "Gay Beach Volleyball." He had never gone before, and I could tell he was going out of his way to help me find community in Santa Cruz. He seemed to feel it was his responsibility, which was very kind but unnecessary. Unfortunately, I am me, and beach volley ball ended up causing me nothing but anxiety. It was on the far beach, close to the amusement park, where several volleyball nets had been set up near the walkway. There was an absurdly giant rainbow flag marking the territory. I knew this was the San Francisco Bay Area, but I still felt vulnerable affiliating myself with the bunch in such an open, day-lit environment. I kept expecting people to jeer at us from the walkway, or throw things, or at the very least laugh. No one appeared to notice us, though. Again, I had the shortest shorts, even with this company.

Lucas talked for a bit with some older gay men he knew- it was mostly older gay men. I forgot that Lucas was in his thirties because he looked much younger. I wondered if that was difficult for him. I wondered whether people disrespected him, interpreting him as a teenage boy even if they knew his age. I knew all too well the burden of being treated as a boy. Lucas was several inches shorter than me, slim, and handsome, with short dirty blonde hair and light blue eyes. He wore mostly baggy, casual clothing. He was a trans guy.

Our house was a small but beautiful bungalow with a stucco tile roof and a general Mission style. There was a small stone patio in the side yard, with a canopy of wood rafters covered in kiwi vines. The front yard had a large palm tree and a garden of cactuses, chipped clay pots, aloe vera, and a Buddha statue. My bedroom was small with only a tiny window, so I usually wrote in the breakfast nook. It was a wonderful home. Lucas had lived there for many years.

Lucas and I didn't talk much around the house. He was usually writing his dissertation in his bedroom- he was working on his PhD. Most our conversations were about cats. Lucas's constant companion was Oliver, a brown tabby who looked a lot like my Tiger, who I had left behind in Syracuse. Unlike Tiger, Oliver was a tough, lean, outdoor cat, adopted from a shelter. It took him several weeks to warm up to me. There were many other cats that visited us, all of whom I named. The regulars were: Boots, a brown Maine Coon with white paws, Whitey, a mean and skittish white shorthair tabby, Fatty Catty, an obese Calico with a purple collar, and Junipurr, a gorgeous, ridiculous gray tabby who showed up the day I arrived and became my companion. They often climbed through the open windows during the day to spend time with us and steal Oliver's food. There were also the backyard cats: several generations of longhaired tabbies who belonged to the people in the in-law apartment attached to our house.

LittleKing wasn't all that attractive in person. I got in his car anyway, and we peeled out of the boardwalk parking lot as the sun was going down. We didn't talk much in the car, and I was pretty detached. I asked him to stop at a gas station, where I picked up a six pack of beer and some cigarettes. Then he drove us to the Seaside Motel.

He complained about girls from the bed as I chugged down the beers. He asked me my name and I told him it was Ell. I stared at the black television. He asked me what I was into.

"Well what would you do if I was a girl?"

I couldn't feel anything, and I had to stop a second after we started. He seemed concerned, but mostly annoyed. I refused his offer of a ride, and I walked home drunk in the dark.

~~~

I lay awake in a San Francisco hotel room in Union Square. It cost me a hundred twenty dollars for a night. What was wrong with me? On an anxious compulsion, I had texted Isaac and announced I was coming in to the city. He expressed that this was pretty sudden and probably not a good idea but... yeah, maybe we could hang out. But I couldn't stay with him. His roommates wouldn't like it. That was fine, I told him, I had other reasons to visit as well. What those reasons were I did not say.

I don't know what came over me. I biked to the bus station where I caught the shuttle to San Jose. The winding roads were horrible on a bus and I spent the entire hour with my eyes closed, trying not to vomit. From San Jose I took the CalTrain to San Francisco, purchasing a hotel room on the way, using my laptop and the free wifi.

I thought, for some reason, if I could just see Isaac in person I could talk sense into him. Here I am: now love me. I knew it was illogical and I wasn't even sure why I wanted this so badly. My general attitude was to follow my whims, lest I someday wonder, "what if?"

I wanted to know I had tried my hardest.

When I got to downtown San Francisco, I stopped in a Walgreens where I picked up some snacks and bottles of champagne. After that, I headed to my hotel room. It was small, but clean and pleasant. One window faced a grey brick wall. The other, the streets with the trolleys. It was very loud. I texted Isaac again to see if he had made up his mind whether he would feel up to getting drinks after work.

> I have some champagne and you can just come here and relax. There's even two beds if you wanna stay over.

I wasn't trying to seduce him- not sexually. Experience told me that alcohol would liberate our conversation and bring us closer. Though I did think that if perhaps we cuddled again, and maybe a kiss occurred, that we would at least have to face the elephant in the room head-on. Not that this had ever been the case in the past. Perhaps his anxious reactions to my advances were actually sensible. I was admittedly trying to corner him.

> I'd rather go out. Do you mind if I invite some friends from work?

I closed my eyes. Really?

I waited a few minutes, then told him I was just going to stay in. Then, against my better judgment, "I don't get it. Are you afraid to see me?"

All in one conversation, Isaac told me we shouldn't hang out, we shouldn't hook up, that he loves me, and that he didn't wish I talked less – he wished he talked more. It was the same night that George Zimmerman was judged not guilty for killing Trayvon Martin. There were riots in Oakland and near Isaac's work. He said there were police helicopters. And for a short moment, I was shaken from my trivial problems and hit with the force of all the injustice and pain in Good old God-save-America. I looked out the window at the street below and I thought, *This must be what the 60's felt like.* But down below people just kept shopping and riding the trolley cars. I was surprised that riding them is free. Someone should be making a lot of money on those…all the white girls in their pea coats holding onto the rail, their friends snapping instagram photos of the adventure. There's nothing wrong with that. That's not what I'm saying.

I'd had way too much champagne. I always had too much champagne. I got pretty drunk and danced around shirtless, singing along to songs on Pandora radio and hugging myself.

I texted,

Of course I am. You're everything I'm attracted to. You're perfect. That's part of what makes this all so difficult for me.

Well OK. I don't mind if we're just friends. I just want to see you, you know?

Maybe we can meet up for mimosas and brunch in the AM?

Just us?

Sure.

Finally!

~~~

Upon being reunited, the following morning, Isaac and I inevitably landed on the topic of our sex lives. We've both had a lot of bad experiences.

"It's different for you, though," I said, scarfing down some nacho potatoes. We were in an Irish pub, or at least a west coast attempt at one. He had work in a half hour. I was pretty drunk, and he seemed intoxicated as well. It was a good drunk for me, though. Silly. "I don't get silly drunk," he had grumbled earlier at the park.

"Because I'm a top and you're a bottom," he said, earnestly, meeting my eyes.

"Yes," I said, "and more so than that, I think we just have different pressures on us. People categorize us differently and have different expectations. I can be feminine as this sort of twinky gay boy and it doesn't invalidate my maleness. I think there is more pressure on you to be masculine, because of your look. I guess *because* you are more masculine, you know? I'm more pretty and little and I fill that role.

I've come to realize I'm fine with my body…I'm a bottom, so what do I really care? Whereas I think it's more complicated for you."

"Yeah," he said, looking sad. I wanted so badly to take his hand. I was just glad to be around him. Much like I had hoped, he really did seem to like me when we actually were face to face. He seemed to value my opinions and to get my personality. He also seemed miserable, but from other things, and eager to confide in me. I really thought it was long-distance communication that was to blame.

Back in Santa Cruz, I lay awake in bed thinking about the sexual experiences Isaac described. I didn't like imagining it. I wasn't jealous or anything, but it caused me pain. It was infuriating to know that stupid men had taken stupid pleasure from his body…his wonderful body that I loved, because it was his, because I loved him, because I felt connected to his body as a transsexual body, like my own. Not a queer body, not a body under the transgender umbrella…a transsexual body. "A product of technology." It's hard to explain.

He was so miserable that day…his body radiated tenseness, anxiety, long-term suffering. He'd always been like this, but…well, it seemed to be getting worse. I was worried. Still, I was so happy to be near him. I thought that if we could always be like we were in Dolores Park, drinking champagne out of red plastic cups, we could be happy together for a very long time indeed.

"Mind if I smoke?" I asked.

"Of course not," he said. He had this brash tone sometimes when he talked to me, but it was affectionate somehow. He looked over as I bent down to get my cigarettes out of the pocket of my backpack. I purposefully angled in hopes that he'll look at my ass. The pack of cigarettes was black and blue with sparkly, silver lettering. "What are those supposed to be?" he said, "Camel Fags?"

I snorted. "Hey fuck you!" I only snort-laugh when I've been around him, because he does it. It's bizarre. I hadn't done it in awhile, but the moment I started walking down the street, he made me laugh and there it was. After spending a week together, it took nearly a month to rid myself of the habit.

"I think about Purchase a lot," he said.

"Me too," I said. "Do you miss it?"

"Strangely, I do. Nothing in our lives will ever be like that again."

"How do you mean?" I asked.

"Well just, all those queer people, gathered in one place, night after night. There was more time, you know? It wasn't just brief meetings between work and sleep. There was time to just exist, for better and for worse. It was like a safety haven in many ways. There was something more authentic about it than living out here. I can't help but romanticize it now."

"I miss it sometimes too," I said. "But I mostly associate it with a lot of painful memories."

"Do you still talk to any of our old friends?"

"Not really.."

"Me neither," he said. "In many ways, you're my closest friend."

We watched dogs chasing one another and sat together like this, just talking and drinking, until it was time for Isaac to go to work. It wasn't enough, and I felt depressed immediately after parting. I then lost my way and spent a good two hours wandering before I found the train station.

~~~

I cried on my second drive from Santa Cruz to San Francisco. A few weeks later I got another rental car and drove up Highway Seventeen, taking all the curves way too fast. "California," came on – the Joni Mitchell song – just as the road straightened out and opened up. The hills rolled out before me, silhouetted with those distinctly northwestern pines on the horizon. I cried because I was strangely happy. Honest to God. I was so happy to be out here, in California, on my way to see one my dearest friends. And that line that always got stuck in my head: *Will you take me as I am?* That's when the tears streamed down my face.

It wasn't just happiness. It was terror as well. Uncertainty. The anticipation. *Will you take me as I am, Will you take me as I am, will you?* It depended on what I meant by that, I guess.

I had a good time in the city that night. Isaac let me stay over with him that time. He was friendly. We didn't end up doing much of anything that we planned – no bars, no meeting up with his friends, just wandering, high, drunk, and talking. I feel like we could talk forever, about being trans, about relationships, loneliness, our pasts, the future, queerness, sex, rage, family, childhood, music, writing, old friends, depression, philosophy, our affection for one another. There was something poignant about walking through the Castro on a Saturday night, high and buzzed and oblivious to all that happened around us. We were too absorbed in our conversations. We must have passed that famous red neon sign three or four times. Otherwise, I would have forgotten we were in the queer capitol of the world. Such was our introversion. Eventually we just wandered home.

We cuddled again that night. I slept in his bed after all. He was exhausted, and so was I, but I couldn't keep my hands to myself. It wasn't sexual. I was just high and scared and in love.

"Isaac, are you awake?" No response. I snuggled up closer. I ran my hand over his chest and stomach. I felt his body hair...his ribs. I gently gripped his bicep. He wasn't particularly muscular or athletic, but he was strong and healthy. I wanted so badly to love him, actively, as a verb...to show that love. I wanted him to want to receive me. I lay my head on his shoulder, and for some reason I thought he was probably only pretending to be asleep.

In the morning, we spooned. I wanted so badly for him to press harder against me, to touch the bare skin of my chest and stomach and more...but that wasn't going to happen. I think that would have qualified as hooking up, even if I was just hands on my body, skin to skin, that I wanted. I think that was too much. I don't think he wanted it, and if he did, he didn't want to want it.

"I can't go there right now," he said, repeatedly. "I need to work on myself. I could tell you all my fucked up therapy stuff but I'll spare you."

But I didn't want to be spared. I wanted to understand.

"I feel like you don't listen to me or respect me," he said.

Why would you think that? I did.

"It's OK that you're so straight forward. But you need to realize not everyone can be like you."

I'm sorry. I was a fool. I just thought you seemed like you felt the same.

"Please don't be embarrassed. We're friends first and I love you."

My mind sorted through all these old text messages, trying to make sense of the mystery. On the phone the next day, Gabe told me he thought Isaac was purposefully fucking with me. I really didn't think so...but I didn't have any better explanation.

~~~

I drove out to San Francisco a third time to bring Isaac back with me to Santa Cruz. I rented the car but let him drive. Everything felt wrong after he told me he thinks he should go back east. I tried to ignore it, but I was terrified at the idea of him leaving. What if I was out here without him? What would I make of it? I tried to push through it, but the day was doomed. We had to have the talk. He took the curves in the road slowly and carefully.

"You need to eat," he told me. "You're too thin."

I laughed it off for a while, but he was serious this time. "That's why you get faint all the time, Elliott. You're destroying your body. You're killing your brain cells. You need to take care of yourself..."

It felt good that he cared.

I was trying, but the mimosas and the cigarettes were all that got me through those long days alone. I didn't want him to feel bad that I felt bad...Honest. I just wished he loved me. That he were in love with me. It wasn't his fault that I was like this. I didn't mean to be. I hated it.

"See, I would take this on as my responsibility," he said. I think he meant if he were dating me, he'd worry about my health. We were high again.

I felt like he was always looking for reasons not to like me. Or to rationalize not liking me, so that he could block me out.

He kept saying he felt calm and great. I felt awful. He kept laughing at the little house I lived in, at the garden gate and the flowers and the stucco roof. "It's just so California!" He said it reminded him of some character from *Mad Men*. Something. I didn't know. Santa Cruz did start to feel like a time warp, stuck in the sixties and seventies. At least what I imagined those decades to feel like. My constantly listening to Joni Mitchell probably added to that illusion.

We ended up in my bedroom. I honest to God just wanted to cuddle. I want to kiss too, always. I always want to kiss him – not necessarily make out, just kiss his lips and face and hands and snuggle up to him. And touch each other...take comfort in each other. Sure. But I wasn't thinking genitals. I wasn't thinking fucking.

"Can I just say something?" he said, as we set up the laptop to watch cartoons or that show he liked, *Kids in the Hall*...I don't remember. "I don't want to hook up, OK? I just want that to be taken off the table, for good." It was sudden and slightly hostile. Perhaps he was finally ripping off the proverbial Band-aid. I felt humiliated.

"Oh...I mean, yeah...OK." I stared at my hands. "I mean, I don't really want to...you mean, never? I'm sorry. I don't know..."

I was too high and there have been too many conversations between us like this. I can't remember it well enough. I don't want to get him wrong. I do remember-

Me: The way I see it, there are two ways I can look at the situation...one is that I like you, and I told you, and you said the feeling was mutual. But you can't be in a relationship right now. In that scenario, I have hope that if I wait...but the second scenario, I told you I like you, but you don't like me in that way and don't want to go there, period.

I: It's complicated and it's a bit of both. But for the sake of how I think you should look at it, it's more the second one.

E: Oh...

I: As time goes on, I realize more and more that my feelings for you really are plutonic.

E: Oh...

(and at some point)

I: I'm not going to be your boyfriend, Elliott.

I knew why they called it heartache, because my chest hurt so badly with embarrassment and loss that I began to cry. He held me, which helped and hurt more. He said he was sorry, he felt bad. We talked about cuddling. He loves cuddling with his friends, he said. I don't cuddle with anybody, I said, self-conscious as my tears and snot dripped on his shirt. He was wearing a plaid shirt over a tank top and this fashion baseball cap of sorts with a unbent rim, cocked slightly to the side. I said something about not knowing how to be friends with men. "We don't need like, a model," he said. He said something about men in Italy, how this is totally normal there, for male friends...and he loves me. I told him something about how lonely I am, how much I want support…somehow it turned into a conversation about how he thinks people project onto him, and how he thinks that I won't want to be friends with him now because he won't have sex with me. That hurt. Does he really think that? After all our conversations? Does he really think I'm that shallow? No, it's his own issues, he knows that…and it's not necessarily *me* he means, it's just that in general, yeah, he really does think that. He feels used by people. I totally wasn't following and felt insulted. I told him so. But at the same time, is his self-esteem really that low? He doesn't think there are things about him that people could find genuinely attractive? His responses are blurs…Why can't I remember things? Because I was high? But I used to be able to remember things anyway, no matter how drugged or drunk. Is it because I don't eat? Is there just too much I'm trying to record?

As if, as if – As if, if I wrote it all down, I could keep him there with me, in those moments, and that would count as something. I could extend his love, plutonic or not, into those lonely hours, alone, in a home that wasn't mine, in a time zone that wasn't mine.

We cuddled a while, but we both thought it was better if he went home earlier than planned. On the drive back we talked even more about being transgender, about always feeling outside of things – I don't know, because I can't remember! I hate forgetting. We talked about…we talked about…

I played "Storms" for him, by Fleetwood Mac. I just had to go there, and I cried, like I knew I would. "That line," I said. "It's how I feel. Not *I try to cry*…No, *my* body *tries to cry.*"

I didn't know what he thought of me in those moments, when I was completely honest and exposed and ridiculous. What kind of man was I? Nearly twenty-five…Who was I modeling myself after? Why did it have to feel like such a joke, being a man who loved men, who listened to Stevie Nicks and Joni Mitchell and Dionne Warwick torch songs? Why did it have to feel so campy, when it was so sincere and so fucking painful?

~~~

I was surprised when I got an invite to Brit's show. We hadn't spoken in years. She was coming to Santa Cruz after playing up north in San Francisco and the East Bay. Maybe it would be good to see her. A part of me thought that maybe, if Isaac came along, the three of us could chill like old times. Maybe a third person would help normalize everything.

I texted Isaac.

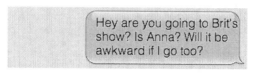

Hey are you going to Brit's show? Is Anna? Will it be awkward if I go too?

He didn't respond, which naturally, by the time a day had passed, made me furious. I eventually texted,

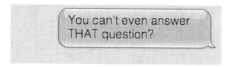

You can't even answer THAT question?

Finally that night I got a long, well-thought out text that read like someone talking slowly to an unstable person holding a gun to his head.

I need significant space from you. Please respect that. The writing you sent me had a very negative effect on me. Anna and I are both planning to go to Brit's show. I really don't want to see you. Please let me know if you are going to show up because I won't go.

I assured him I wasn't going. I couldn't believe this tone he was taking. Was he seriously afraid of me? Sure, I was little messed up. I was sad about him, and was never the happiest guy to begin with. But did my behavior really warrant this kind of caution and aversion?

Later I got an email from one of the lesbians getting married. A smaltzy, passive-aggressive email.

> "Hi Elliott, I hope you are well. You see as a wedding party-type thing we were all going to Brit's show and it's very important to me. For obvious reasons it would be uncomfortable if you were there, so if you plan on going will you please give me a head's up? Thank you so much."

I refused to respond to that. I was back at SUNY Purchase, when everyone hated me, when Isaac got away with fucking me behind Anna's back and fucking us both over and then even fucking another guy pretty much right in front of us at a party. Isaac was never anything but a victim in all of it and I was a bitchy, obsessive, depressing monster. I was once again uninvited to the cool kids' party. Fuck that.

I used to feel guilty about the implications in *Refuse* as to the character of the company I kept in college. I didn't anymore. There was no loyalty or honesty among them. I knew I did a bad thing to Anna, and I apologized several times. No one had ever apologized to me. No one ever really cared. I wanted nothing to do with any of them. This fury mixed with my fury for San Francisco, downstate New York, Brooklyn, upper-middle class hipster queers. Fury for being fired, for all the fucked up men I'd fucked, for all that I would never experience. All the pent up frustration, my overwhelming desire to love and succeed and please, and the overwhelming disappointment I faced again, and again, and again...

Fuck it. I was going home.

~~~

I sat outside smoking in the yard. Lucas had the door to his room open, and I sort of hoped he'd come out. I was sitting in his ripped-up old camp chair with an end table I use for a writing desk. A mimosa was perched on its corner.

Lucas emerged from his room with his skateboard. "How's it going?" he asked.

"Um...not so great," I said, the alcohol making me honest.

"Oh how come?" He set his skateboard down and sat on the step.

"Just trying to figure shit out," I said.

"Are you worried about going back to Syracuse?"

"A little, but it's not that. It's more to do with my writing."

"Like what you're currently working on?"

"Yes. See, it's weird. What I'm writing is sort of nonfiction now, and I gave it to a person...well, Isaac – " I introduced the two of them a few weeks prior, the one time Isaac had visited all summer. "—And he read some of it. A lot of it is about him...it's not really a memoir because I'm writing it as it's happening. It's a really strange thing. The first part I sent him he really loved. He said it was beautiful, that it made him cry- and he's not a big crier- that I'm writing about important thing in a raw, honest way. He compared it to James Baldwin. He was really complimentary and it felt really meaningful. Particularly because he added, "I love you, Elliott." But the second installment upset him and I don't know why. He won't explain. He just doesn't want to see me or talk to me anymore."

"Did it portray him in a negative light?"

"I mean, I don't think so? Admittedly, the second document was the stuff I was worried to send him the first time. But I reread it all and I really don't know what upset him so much. It just made me feel really awful. He said he needed *serious space.* And that my writing *scared* him. What does that even mean? It makes me feel like he thinks I'm crazy or something. I mean yeah, I express strong emotions in my writing, but I'm not unstable or anything."

"Did you ask him what he meant?"

"Yeah, but he takes ages to respond to texts or just doesn't at all. I waited about ten minutes, and normally I know that isn't long, but in his case, I knew he was done. Because he does it all the time. Sometimes he'll respond a day later, sometimes never."

"I guess I do that sometimes too, when I'm busy," Lucas said. "But not with my close friends."

"I know. See I feel like I sound obsessive when I say it aloud. But he does it in a way that really gets to me. I know he is purposefully avoiding talking to me and I don't get why it's so hard to respond. It's an ongoing thing and it's really inconsiderate. And then he acts like I'm dramatic when I get upset about it."

"Yeah...he sounds high maintenance."

"He is! He's so easily freaked out by the littlest thing. It's as if he's always on the border of a panic attack and it's somehow my fault. And see, I would have taken the hint months ago if it weren't for the fact that when we actually hang out, we have a good time. We really connect. And he would always say he loved me. He would text *I love you*. And it was in intense contexts, you know? So I asked him if he meant it in as more than friend love...because it seemed like it. And he says, *can I have some time to think about that?* As if I asked him to write an essay and he needs an extension."

"But you really like him - You love him."

"I...don't know anymore. I don't know. I feel like we do have something special, despite it all. It's hard to explain. I feel disconnected and connected to him at the same time. But it's pointless carrying this torch for him."

"I get that...It's kind of different, but my ex was really awful to me after we broke up last year. He slashed my tires, he threatened me and my friends...but I still feel this weird bond with him that I don't feel with anyone else. It's probably because he's trans, and he was one of the first trans men I really got to know."

"That's how Isaac is for me too," I said. "Have you ever read the Sherlock Holmes stories?"

"Um...not really," Lucas said.

"Well, there's one where this woman outsmarts him. And even though Sherlock Holmes is basically asexual, from that point on, he referred to her as The Woman. As if she were the only one. And that's how I've thought of Isaac- He's *The Trans Man.*"

"Personally, I just try to keep my ex in a box now," Lucas said. "This very specific place so that he never gets too close."

We were silent and pensive for a bit.

"It probably was dramatic to tell him to forget me," I said. "But I didn't know what else to do. I asked him to explain, I told him I had no idea what he was talking about...I told him I don't get why he always acts to fragile. That was mean. That probably bothered him a lot. I don't know. I just said, *You know what? You make me feel like shit. Forget it. I won't ever bother you or scare you or stress you out again. I'm deleting your number, I'm leaving California anyway, just forget about me entirely.*" I stared down at my hands, feeling tears behind my eyes. A part of me thought, *As if he could ever forget me.* Another part thought *as if he thinks about you anyway.*

Eventually, Isaac did block me out. He wouldn't respond to anything, even when I tried to explain I only wanted to preserve a friendship at this point...and well, that was that. It occurred to me that he may have shared my writing with Anna, despite that when he asked whether he could, I said no. Perhaps they decided together that I was crazy and awful. It hurt, because among what I sent him was some of the most vulnerable pieces I'd ever written. I'd never find out what was so horrible about them.

I knew he'd never reach out to me. Unless I initiated it, it would be years until we talked again. Actually, we probably wouldn't. He wouldn't fight for my friendship. He would never experience that moment in which, one night, standing in the kitchen after pouring himself a glass of water, looking out the window at a crescent moon, he would think, "You know, Elliott may not be perfect, but he really cared for me. He was a good person despite his sadness. He really loved me. I bet he's really hurting and would feel better if I just gave him a call..." I wanted so badly for that to happen, but it never would.

"It sounds like you were really hurt," Lucas said. There was a tender simplicity to it. I was struck by how kind he seemed in that moment. As if kindness was this rare, rare quality in men. Maybe it is.

"Yeah," I said. "I really was."

I <3 fem/trans

About ⌄
Heteroflexible - usually straight but shit happens

Looking For
Chat, Dates, Friends, Networking, Relationship

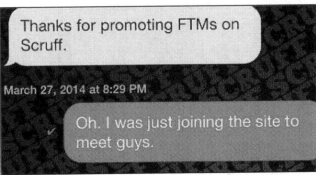

Thanks for promoting FTMs on Scruff.

March 27, 2014 at 8:29 PM

Oh. I was just joining the site to meet guys.

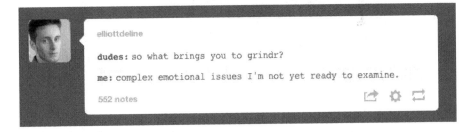

elliottdeline

dudes: so what brings you to grindr?

me: complex emotional issues I'm not yet ready to examine.

552 notes

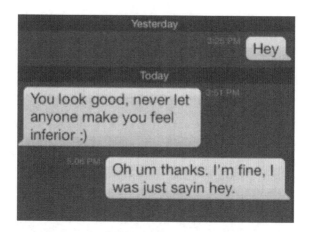

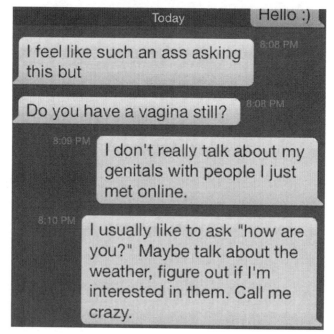

Monday
11:49 PM
Wow! You very impressive trans! Very handsome!)))

Yesterday
4:43 PM
I'm a show trans.

6:40 PM
Oh wow. Very kool!)))

Today
9:25 AM
I was being sarcastic. Like a show dog. Because you're patronizing me. Bye.

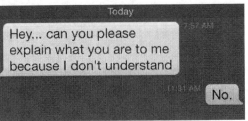

Today
7:57 AM
Hey... can you please explain what you are to me because I don't understand

11:31 AM
No.

elliottdeline

My life is so bizarre

I'm in the waiting room for a very uncomfortable doctor's appointment. I'm going to have to out myself to the doctor and hope for the best. I've got back up. In the waiting room, a woman on the phone is talking loudly. She had an argument last night with her boyfriend about whether playing with barbies would make her 2 year old son "a fag." I can't even.

Another slightly horrifying tale of gay online dating

Last night I started talking to this guy who lives a little north of here. Physically, he was very attractive to me. His profile was pretty sparse but he liked the outdoors and the vague "music and movies" so OK, maybe. His profile, as well as mine, state that we are looking for a relationship and dating, not anonymous sex. We confirmed this with the typical, "so what are you looking for?" exchange. He says to me, "I like that you're thin. That's something I look for, along with a good personality." I blinked a few times and then decided to take it in the best light. I mean everyone has a type. I personally liked that he was muscular and shaved his head, so that's fine. I joked, "Oh well I hope I don't put on weight before I meet you then." I hoped to hear that he wouldn't care. "Ur funny," he said. Strike 1. We exchanged numbers. Or numbs, as he called it. Strike 2.

We texted a bit but I fell asleep on the couch watching the snow. I woke up and saw he sent me a shirtless photo and has asked me to send him another photo. He is sort of flipping out. "What do you think? Not interested? Ehhhhhhh..." Strike 2 and 1/2. I told him he's hot, I was just napping and I sent him a photo of me. Clothed. That's how I roll.

He says, "You're cute. You look pretty thin." Yeah...we covered that already. It was starting to seem weird.

"So tell me about yourself," he said. I was a little grumpy, but honest, and said, "I'd rather just talk in person. Do you want to get something to eat some time?" He said definitely. But then, "Sorry if this is weird, but can you send me a pic of your stomach or something? I want to see how thin you are." Strike 3.

I told him that honestly, that was kinda weird and that I didn't like the idea of him judging whether I was thin enough to go out with him. He said, "I don't judge, I just like to get everything out in the open before we meet. You don't seem to want to talk or show me what you look like but I would rather know first." To reiterate, I sent him perfectly fine photos with my face and body, just wearing a tee shirt and shorts. So he could even see my friggin legs. "I mean you're the only person who finds it weird," he said. "Be real, if I was fat you wouldn't have messaged me." I told him I was actually more attracted to muscular stocky guys over thin guys and that chubby definitely wasn't a turn off. "Well I prefer skinny," he said. At that point, I blocked his number. Strangely, my trans status never came up.

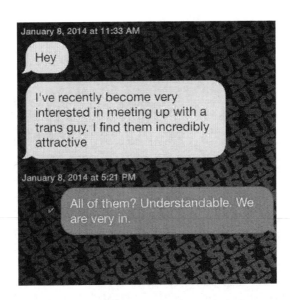

elliottdeline

OKCupid: Off to a good start for 2014

Dude: Hi, I liked your profile. We apparently aren't a good match and don't have a lot in common but I'd still like to talk. I'm not a vegetarian- I do like animals, I just also like eating them. I'm not a cat person either. They just always have that bitchy, I'm-gonna-smack-you-in-the-face look that I don't trust...

Me:

Yeah I don't think it's gonna work out.

7 notes

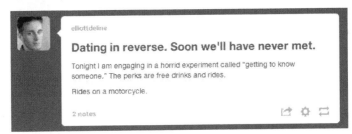

elliottdeline

Dating in reverse. Soon we'll have never met.

Tonight I am engaging in a horrid experiment called "getting to know someone." The perks are free drinks and rides.

Rides on a motorcycle.

2 notes

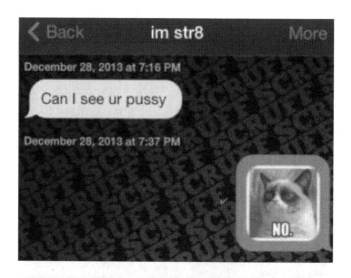

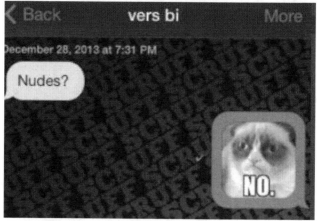

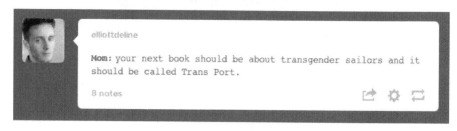

March 22, 2014 at 11:27 PM

Hi sexy nipple

elliottdefine

More adventures in online dating

Cis dude: It takes a lot of courage. Good luck to you.

Me: Thanks.

Cis: Your welcome

Me: You mean being transgender?

Cis: Yes

Me: Oh. Well it doesn't really take courage. It's just how I am. Nothing more to it than that.

Cis: Well I'm sure it has to be the greatest journey it does take a lot of courage to be happy with yourself

Me: No, it's kind of sucked honestly.

Cis: sorry dude

#i probably should be nicer   #but i just don't care   #THE GREATEST JOURNEY!!1!

1 note

111

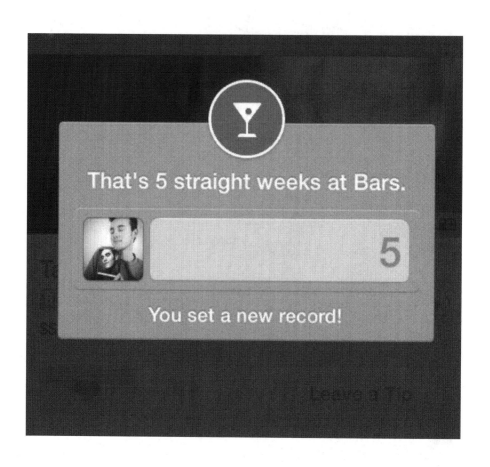

Part Four

A few months later I was once again searching "FTM" on the Syracuse craigslist and who do I come across but Michael. He was looking specifically for trans guys. He said he hooked up with one before and it was one of the best experiences of his life. Really? Because for me, it was hell. At least the repercussions were hell. I don't know. It was sort of flattering still.

We met up again. I don't even remember the first time. I don't think I even drank. I don't need to, I just black it all out anyway. It's horrible. We hooked up five or six times over the next few weeks, probably using protection less than half the time. I told him that we needed to. I told him it was hard for me to assert this desire in person, especially when drunk, but we needed to. Otherwise we needed to stop hooking up. "Yeah that's cool," he'd say in a text, only to make me play condom-police in the bedroom. "Alright," he'd sigh, "But I don't have any Magnums. These ones are too small and uncomfortable." Give me a break.

We got drinks one night at an Irish bar downtown. He picked me up in the same flashy car. At the bar, he introduced me to his straight dude friends from the NAVY. I don't think they know he sleeps with guys. He said he preferred women anyway, and for some reason that was appealing to me. I wanted him to want me like he would want a woman. Kind of. His friends could be described as having "booming" voices. I felt extraordinarily effeminate, and not even in the typical sense. At least most fags are loud and showy. There's at least something intimidating in that.

Michael bought me drinks. We got talking about stuff. I loosened up. We shot some pool, played a game of darts. We talked about what happened last time- the whole STD thing. He told me he had changed and was looking for a regular friend with benefits or a relationship. He told me he was clean, hadn't had sex in five months, and was recently tested. "You know what," I thought. "What the hell. I trust him." See for him, condoms made it not *feel* as good. He lost his erection. Poor dear, I knew I was already difficult enough. I'd say I'm coming over but then I'd change my mind. I'd feel guilty about the sex and stop answering his texts for a few days. I'd have to stop in the middle of sex because I was dissociating again. And on top of all that, I'm trans. Confusing, gross, easily offended and trans. Poor Michael. I said, "Hey, don't worry about it. It's fine. I believe you."

Trust kills. Literally.

The sex got better. I started using my words- something that's really hard for me. I lingered in the bed a bit instead of running away. We…talked. I wasn't in love, but I was at least growing fond of him. I liked sitting around drinking and watching TV. We watched a lot of dumbass guy TV. Stuff about cops and high-speed chases. It made me feel like such a girl. Strangely, I liked that.

Do you watch football at all

Haha no

Another time,

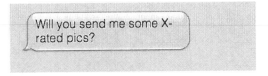

He was the much coveted "masc" man. Masc for fem. Who knew they existed?

He told me about the shooting techniques in the military versus how the police do it ("See, they run and *then* they shoot, as opposed to shooting *while* they run. That's why so many cops get killed). He had this amazing plum wine one night and I drank most of it. The next time he mixed Amaretto with vodka and rum. It was horrible but he guilted me. "That's some expensive liquor you're wasting." I *did* say I wanted a drink. I *did* invite myself over. Poor Michael. I gulped it down then let him fuck me bareback despite my earlier protests.

I liked the dynamic at times. He found me weird, yet it seemed to amuse him. "Hooking up with you is always an experience," he'd say, shaking his head. He was always complimenting me too. "You look good in pink," or, "Your ass is so fine."

~~~

One morning, I woke up and immediately knew something was wrong down there. Shit. I didn't even know where to go. I wanted this gone, pronto, but was ashamed to see my doctor again. He basically scolded me last time. I couldn't even consider going back to the anonymous clinic after how they treated me. You make certain resolutions, but then you get to know somebody over drinks. You start to let your guard down. You open up just a little and that's all it takes. Viruses flood in. The human body's a real bitch like that.

I called my doctor anyway, just in case. I lied to the woman on the phone about why I was calling. I said I have a sore throat. What was I supposed to say? "There's a problem with my vagina," in my baritone voice? She said the nurse would get back to me. But I realized I don't want this showing up on my parents' insurance.

Finally Gabe got off work and took me to the Q Center at ACR- the queer youth center. A man was there, George. He's cisgender, but he's sat in on the trans group a few times. He's got a beard and a ponytail and a laid back vibe.

"Maybe you can help me," I said. And I explained to him my situation. He told me I could go to the basement of the Civic Center and it'd be anonymous. But that was where I went last time and was basically yelled at for being transgender. Apparently the staff at the Q Center went to that place to teach transgender sensitivity. And George offered to go in with me on Monday, to make sure they didn't give me trouble. I just had to get through the weekend.

Even infected, Michael and I met up that night. He was eating pizza and watching *Family Guy* with two white, frat boy-type friends. I doubted these were the dudes from his biker gang. They seemed to fresh-faced. They didn't seem like military guys either. Who were these people? Oh, and yes, Michael had a biker gang. They weren't criminals, just dudes who rode together and did all kinds of other shit. I didn't really listen much when he told me about it.

Michael was tough. He was the kind of guy who punched people in bars. I have a thing for those types of guys. Why? Punching people was fine, but I had a bad feeling about the way he treated his pit bull, Roxanne. She always cowered in his presence, tail between her legs, trying to sneak over to snuggle up to me and lick my face. "Roxanne, enough!" he'd yell, no matter how many times I told him I liked her attention. He'd smack her butt and tell her to go lie in her kennel. "She's jealous of you," he told me. I didn't know what to make of that. He was wrong of course. Roxanne and I got each other.

"If she ever so much as snarls at me I'm gonna throw her back in the pound," he told me once, which seemed bizarre because she seemed completely submissive and tame. Eventually he replaced her with a male.

I parked my car and put money in the meter, then took my time walking to the STD clinic. I was still a bit early for meeting George. Downtown Syracuse is certainly not as busy as other cities, but it's got a pulse. Syracuse always seems most itself, most alive, in the early winter. December, as it was, before Christmas. We complain, but we secretly thrive in the cold and the snow, like arctic creatures. We take pride in our ability to keep things running despite the accumulation. Every year, we cross our fingers, hoping to win the national record for annual snowfall. We usually do, occasionally beat out by Buffalo or Erie, Pennsylvania or some shit in North Dakota.

Much of Syracuse appears to have been untouched for about sixty years—and not especially well preserved, but still beautiful to me. While I despair over the hardships of our city, I dread the day we enter the twenty-first century and replace everything with modern monstrosities. Some architecture is newer, particularly around the university, but over all, it's a hodgepodge of peeling paint, red bricks, and rusting iron ranging from the eighteen to nineteen seventies. The Erie Canal used to run straight through the heart of city. Now there's a noisy highway.

Past cathedrals and the statues I went, to the Civic Center, a building that functions as many things. I went there with my dad to see the Nutcracker when I was little. It was a yearly trip around the holidays. Our "father daughter date."

I went down the steps to the dreaded "Room 8," where George was waiting for me outside.

"My client is transgender," I heard George tell the blonde, middle-aged woman at the desk.

"Oh that's fine!" she said in an unnaturally high-pitched voice.

I couldn't hear what George said next.

The woman said, "Why doesn't he just tell us?"

"He's very nervous."

I wish George had mentioned it was because I had faced discrimination there in the past. Instead he made me sound like a squirmy puppy. He motioned me to come forward. I had to sign paperwork.

"Could I have a key for the bathroom?" I asked the receptionist. I made a conscious effort to make eye contact and to not look ashamed.

"Yep," she said loudly, "Same key for everybody. Man, woman, transgender, whatever!" The other woman sitting further back in the room gave me an undisguised glare.

"Thanks," I said, taking the key.

"So why are you here?" The nurse asked me.

I explained to her that I believed I had an STD, that I had unprotected sex, and I read online and I fit the symptoms.

"What symptoms?" she asked, picking up a pen.

"Well first off, I need you to know that I am transgender. From female to male. So my body—"

"So which parts do you have?" she asked, her tone harsh, cutting me off mid-sentence.

"If I may finish," I said, "I have had chest reconstruction and I am on testosterone. I have female reproductive organs."

"So you have a vagina?" She said.

I frowned. "Yeah."

"And what are the symptoms?"

I told her.

"And do you plan to have surgery to get a penis?"

"I don't really see how that is relevant to today's examination," I said. I was proud of myself.

She looked flustered, "Oh well if you were we would need to have you change your sex in the system. And then you would have a blue form instead of the pink."

119

I stared at my hands, but persisted. "Can't we just deal with that if it happens?"

"Of course, of course," she said.

Wow.

She took my blood to test for a couple things, including HIV. I told her I preferred a urine test for gonorrhea and clamydia.

"We don't do those," she said. "We do the swab test."

"I'm not comfortable with that," I said. "I know that you do the urine test, because I came here once before and they assumed I was male and asked for my urine."

"We only do urine for males. If you get surgery and we change your sheet, then you can do the urine test."

"I read online that it doesn't matter which sex, you can pick up on it in urine."

She eventually gave in and let me do a urine test and then a swab test myself, which she took to a lab. When she came back, she already had a diagnosis. A text message for Michael later confirmed that he had received the same news.

Within a few days of treatment, I was feeling back to my normal self. But I told Michael that from this point forward, we needed to tell one another if we were with someone else, and we were always using protection. He said sure.

Within a few days, I was free of all symptoms and hanging out with Michael again.

I typed the rest of my explanation, pressed send, then bit my lip, waiting.

He didn't say anything to this, which I interpreted as unenthusiastic acceptance.

~~~

Michael gave me more plum wine. It was super sweet and easy to get carried away. He had two friends there that night from his motorcycle club. When he spoke of them, I had been picturing this group as either older black thug types or white men who looked like they belonged on *Duck Dynasty.* These two were just dudes, like frat boys but rougher around the edges. Both were white, shorter and smaller than Michael, dressed in jeans and hoodies and baseball caps. My drunkenness and indifference made them seem identical to me. They were drinking vodka straight and smoking weed. No one offered me any.

I sat in the recliner while the three of them lounged out on the couch watching *Family Guy.* They had a pepperoni pizza on the coffee table in front of them. I nibbled on a breadstick between sips of wine. I hadn't been expecting his friends to be there and I was a little annoyed. However, it wasn't long before one of them passed out. The other friend thought this was hilarious.

"He was the one who wanted to drink," he kept repeating. "He thinks he can handle so much but he can't. He seriously had like four drinks."

Another half hour passed. I was checking my phone and thinking of leaving when the second friend said, "Can I go lie down in your room for a bit? I've got work in the morning."

"Yeah, take the guest room," Michael said. "If you pass out, you can just stay the night. It's cool."

After his friend staggered off to the guest room, Michael sat watching television a little longer. He changed the channel to the show he always watched. He recorded it on his DVR. It was like America's Funniest Home videos for eighteen to twenty-four year old guys. They found videos on YouTube.

"Who is that guy anyway?" I asked, meaning the host of the program.

"You don't *know*?" Michael went on to tell me how the guy was some skateboarder who came from a blue-collar family and worked his way up to becoming a famous skater and inventing a sneaker company. It was a dull story but it seemed to mean a lot to him.

"I'm gonna go to the bathroom," I said. I didn't actually have to go. Instead, I went into his bedroom and lay down in his bed.

I closed my eyes, and pretended to be asleep. Thirty seconds or so later, the door creaked open and Michael crept inside. I heard him removing his dog tags, like usual. Then he got into the bed. I remained motionless, eyes closed, breathing slowly and audibly through my nose. With the blinds closed, it was so dark that even when I opened my eyes for a second, I couldn't see him right in front of me.

He lay down next to me on the right. That was always his side. Same with Isaac. Why? Maybe it's more accurate to say that my side is on the left. At least in both case, my side is by the wall. I like to be by the wall.

Michael began touching my body under my shirt. It was still a thrill to have my chest exposed to someone and touched. It really made me conscious of the surgery's effect. Otherwise I often forgot about it and took it for granted. I kept pretending to be asleep, like we had planned. I was enjoying myself more than ever. I felt relaxed. Perhaps it was the lack of pressure to act, and therefore the lack of opportunity to make a fool of myself. For instance, the prior time I accidentally kneed Michael in the balls.

"I'm sorry," I repeated a dozen times.

"It's okay," he said. "Women tend to forget those are there..."

I lay with my back to him for a minute or so while he recovered.

"Okay," he eventually said, "Wanna keep going?"

"I need a minute," I said, staring at the wall.

"Okay."

"I'm not a woman," I said.

"What?"

"I'm not a woman. You said women tend to forget, and I'm just saying that I'm not a woman."

Michael scoffed. "Oh, well you know what I meant."

No. See this is the part where you apologize.

"I knew what you meant," I said, "But I'm not a woman."

Michael had rustled around a bit by the bed stand, I assumed securing the necessary supplies. I was still pretending to be asleep, as planned, and every sensation was heightened to a pleasurable maximum when he entered me. What followed was incredible. I didn't feel close to him or anything like that, but it didn't matter. That was never what it was about. It was about complimentary projections, compatible fetishes found in one another. I didn't feel affection but I felt validated, deserving, and secure in my pleasure. There was no gender, because there was no ego. Only id on id.

I had the desire to touch his penis. I never did this, with my hand or mouth. It was too much. I think this annoyed him, but I couldn't ever bring myself to do it. But I wanted to suddenly, and I did. I immediately discovered he wasn't wearing a condom. Shocked, I lay back again on the pillows, allowing him to continue, drifting away in my mind. Then,

"Okay, stop. Stop. I need you to stop."

Over the next few days, I felt my anger rising as I pieced together what had happened. He would deny it of course. He would say he didn't know, but he did. He would say I wasn't clear enough, but I was. I felt violated and betrayed. All the old baggage started coming back- all those helpless feelings of exhaustion and depression, slight depravity, and victimhood. Ultimately, I sent him a text message explaining why we were through, and didn't wait for his reply before blocking him, and saving his number as "STDs! Do Not Text Drunk Or Ever!" which now appeared right above, "Stop Texting, He Won't Respond, You're Too Good For Him, Not Even That Cute," who of course was Isaac.

~~~

Several boxes, addressed to me, arrived at my parents' house around the same time. All my belongings had already been shipped back from Santa Cruz months ago, so there was no doubt in my mind as to what these packages contained. I made some vague, would-be explanation and rushed with them up to my bedroom. I hid the contents until the entire ensemble had arrived.

Grey knit stockings, knee-length, covered my hairy legs. I shaved my face bare while looking in a hand mirror. It took a surprisingly long time- I usually just trim it to leave stubble. I shakily traced my lower eyelid with a dark make-up pencil and then closed my eyes and shaded my upper eyelid with some weird brownish color- it was all I could find lying around the house. I applied purplish red lipstick, then rubbed my lips together and dabbed at them with a tissue. This was the only part I vaguely remembered my mother teaching me. I was only guessing at everything else. I applied a little rouge to my cheeks as well. It didn't look great but it wasn't horrible.

Next I undressed and put on the undergarments. Black, lace panties with red trim and an open crotch. There were little red bows that I quickly cut off with scissors. Then the lace bra, very similar in color scheme. It wouldn't have fit me even before I'd had surgery. Exaggeration was a reoccurring element in my fantasies. I put the fake foam breasts in each cup. After I pulled on a tight white tank top, they looked quite real.

I put on a pair of shorts that I had bought that summer. They were unisex, and were very short if I wore them up above my bellybutton on my waist. I then removed the wig from the package. It was a cheap Halloween one, but it did the trick. The plastic hairs were brown, with a feathered style and long bangs that covered my eyebrows and fell into my eyes. I ran my fingers though it until it looked right.

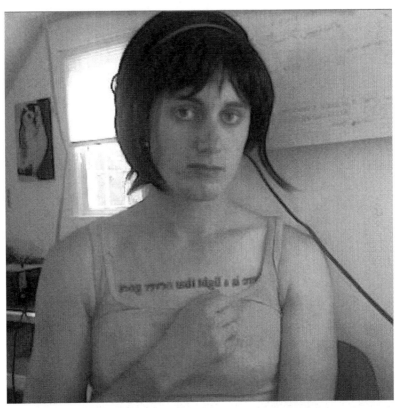

In the mirror, I saw what perhaps, once, had been my worst fear: I was a sexually attractive girl. In fact, I was a little taken aback. I'd never tried to look sexy, except as a boy and a man, and those were very different matters. The hairstyle complimented my features much like I had suspected. I was impressed with my figure. I actually had an ass. My stomach was quite toned. I was getting aroused. Was I a transvestite?

The urge to do this had come on rather suddenly and had been urgent. Why now? Why was this so gratifying? Did I need an answer? Why over-think it?

I took off the shorts once more. Slowly, the rest of it came off and naked, I was a boy again. Female-to-male crossdresser. Why not? I put all of it back in a cardboard box that I hid in my closet. I got back into my jeans and sweatshirt and curled up in my bed, making the split complete: sexual female, asexual male. My sexual self was a persona. It had nothing to do with Elliott. It was a game to play and nothing more. Temporarily comforted by these thoughts, I took a nap.

~~~

I got off the highway at 7th North Street and following Rick's directions, found his small house. I sat in the driveway for several minutes with the engine still running before texting him, "I'm here." When I got to the door, he was already waiting for me.

Rick was an obese man with blond hair and a goatee, and probably in his thirties or so. He wore glasses and a dumpy gray sweatshirt. He introduced himself and shook my hand. His kitchen was full of dirty dishes and empty bottles and cans.

"So yeah," he said, "As you can see, plenty of work to be done. But tonight we will just get to know one other."

A floral sheet separated the living room off from the kitchen. He led me through it, to a couch where we sat. He was watching *The Daily Show with Jon Stewart*. When I settled in to my seat, he handed me a bowl and a lighter, as promised.

"So you're unemployed," he said. "That's rough man."

I nodded, inhaling the smoke.

"I was unemployed for two years," he said. "It's rough out there nowadays. I feel for you. You know how many jobs I applied for?"

I didn't say anything.

"One thousand, four hundred and seven," he said. "Can you believe that?"

I didn't.

"Now I repair computers. I sort of have my own business on the side. I went to school for architecture though. What a waste of time that was."

I didn't say anything.

"How old are you?" he asked.

I cleared my throat. "I'm twenty-five."

"I'm thirty-two," Rick said. "Time flies."

I nodded, bored. I was starting to feel high, and nothing really mattered.

"So I guess what you can do is clean the kitchen, the bathroom, vacuum…" Rick sort of gestured around the room. "Not too much work really. Maybe a couple hours, a few times a week."

I kept nodding, watching the TV. Then, rather suddenly, panic set in. Where even was I? Liverpool? Salina? The North Side? How had I gotten there? Was texting Gabe Rick's contact info really enough? I had mentioned this to Rick, pointedly: that a friend knew where I was and was waiting to hear back from me. That wouldn't stop him from raping or robbing me though. He might not even believe me. He could be a serial killer. Was this really worth the money? No. I knew it wasn't. There was more to it than that. It was the craving to feel desirable. But I only felt worse. How many times would I put myself on the line like this? How many times had I already? I lost track. My memories were fuzzy at best. It was as if different encounters happened to separate people, with separate timelines, who could only communicate so much through the haze. Why was there so much haze? The weed was clouding the dingy room, but it was more than that. I couldn't remember who I even was.

"I have to go," I said, getting to my feet and putting on my jacket.

127

"Oh," Rick said, looking disappointed. "Well OK. Is everything alright?"

"Yeah, it's nothing personal," I said, "It's just something that happens. I get weird."

"Yeah. I understand. I should have mentioned that is strong stuff."

"It's fine," I said.

"Should I contact you?" Rick said.

I stopped, staring at the TV and holding my coat. Several minutes passed. I was floating away, practically asleep standing up. I was very, very high. Moving seemed like a bad idea.

"Uhh…" Rick scratched his head, looking uncomfortable.

"I can't decide what to do," I said.

"I understand," he said, "It can be tough to make decisions."

I wondered whether he meant when you're high or just in general. I didn't ask.

"Why don't you just dust before you go," Rick said, reaching over and grabbing a feather duster from the coffee table. "Just for a bit. Then I'll give you some gas money, alright?"

"Okay," I said, taking the duster from the coffee table.

"And take off your clothes," Rick added, leaning back in his chair and unzipping his pants. He pulled up Xtube on the television, and scrolled through amateur solo videos of FTMs who were much more hairy and masculine than me. "What are you into?" he asked.

"Not this," I said. "Nothing like this. Anything but this. Straight people."

I was naked now, and dusting the television stand and speakers half-heartedly. Rick was staring between my legs

"Why don't you dust under the DVD player?" Rick said. "Get down on your hands and knees…yeah just like that. Arch your back a little, baby…yeah…just like that…"

When I left a few hours later, Rick handed me some bills. "For the cleaning," he said. "I don't pay for sex. Never have, never will."

I nodded and left. When I got to the car, I blocked his number in my phone so that I wouldn't need to hear how much fun he had and how sexy he found my pussy. I could tell I let him fuck me, but I couldn't remember it happening.

I closed my eyes and stroked the stubble on my face. I decided I wanted to let my body hair grow back. There was comfort in masculinity. I wished I were twenty years older—graying, distinguished, like Morrissey on the cover of *You Are the Quarry*. Surely this would pass with age. Surely this was something I just needed to work through: my "lady problem." But at the moment, the pain and the shame was eating away at me. I looked in the rearview mirror. My temples were starting to go gray, a few hairs at a time. There was hope. Or did that just make it all the more pathetic?

I turned on the ignition. The radio was left on 92.1, or Oldies 92.

"If you're going to San Francisco

Be sure to wear some flowers in your hair

If you're going to San Francisco

You're gonna meet some gentle people there."

I laughed to myself as I started the car and backed out of the driveway. The sound of the radio was full of static now, cutting in and out:

"For fshshshshhhhhhhhshhhh San Francisco

Summertime fshshshshshhh love shhhhhhsh

In the streets of shhhhhhshshhhhhsh

Gentle people with flowers in their fshshhhhhshhhhh."

As I pulled onto the 81 North ramp, I recalled how Isaac would say he was changing, and that he was working on himself. I wondered how that was going. I wondered if anyone ever really changed. Then again, maybe the real challenge was staying the same. Sticking with something. Sitting still. Staying true.

I still had a long way to go. The winds would pick up once more and carry me away from here. But for now, I was alright driving on route 81 and watching the sun set. Behind abandoned buildings, church steeples, and fading billboards, there was a golden light as the sun set. At moments like this, driving home on route 81, I could swear Syracuse was the most beautiful city in the world.

~~~

The man across the table from me had a shaved head, probably to hide the fact that he was balding. That's generally why white men do that, unless they are skinheads. He wasn't bad looking, though he was significantly older than me. It was hard to read what sort of guy he was. Well-dressed enough, with designer jeans and a leather jacket. He seemed gay, but from what I could tell he wasn't. I sipped my tea out of a Styrofoam cup. We were the only people in Dunkin Donuts this time of night. Even the staff seemed to have disappeared.

"So did you get a lot of responses?" he asked.

"Kinda," I said, running my fingers though my hair. "I guess so. Yeah."

"So…why house cleaning?"

"Heh, uh…well…" I took a sip of tea. It wasn't that I got a bad vibe from this guy. But I didn't get a good vibe either. "I don't know. I mean…It doesn't have to be house cleaning."

He didn't seem to understand. "So what do you do?" He probably assumed that the car I'd driven there was mine. He must have thought I had money. Otherwise, why ask what I do? Wouldn't it seem I was doing what I did?

"I work for a non-profit and at a youth center," I said. It wasn't a lie. I was volunteering at the Q Center, after school and facilitating a trans youth group. I was also a driving force behind a local group called CNY for Solidarity. As of a few days prior, it was a licensed, incorporated non-profit. I just didn't get paid for any of this. I learned the hard way never to mention that I write.

"That's cool," he said, though he obviously couldn't care less.

130

"Thanks." Why did they always have to ask questions? Couldn't they see I was trying not to be a person?

"So you're transgender," he said. "That's one of the reasons I contacted you. I guess I just liked the way your ad was written. I find transgender people...not *fascinating*. That's not the word I want. Well, yeah, I guess it is. I find them pretty fascinating."

"Oh," I said.

"So you don't mind if I ask questions, do you?"

"No," I said. "Well, not most questions."

"So do you mostly date men, women...?"

"Men," I said. "I used to date women. But now I'm more interested in men." I spoke in a monotone, avoiding his eyes. "What about you?" I asked this innocently enough, but it carried a slight threat. It implicated him.

"What? Women!" He didn't reveal any anger, only surprise.

"I just thought I'd ask."

He let it go. "And how long since you made the change?"

I hated that. Why did they always call it that? *Making the change.* "I started hormone therapy a little over five years ago."

"Oh, okay."

We sat for a few moments in silence.

"So you seem sane," I said.

"Probably too sane," he said. "I'm boring."

"No, you're fine," I said, though I sort of agreed. "Are you good? Do you wanna go back to your place now?"

"You know," he said. "I...Ha. I'm just not feeling it."

"Oh," I said. My heart plummeted. "Oh, alright. You can just go if you want."

"Yeah, I think we're both just kind of awkward at this. I'm just not feeling it. But look, here's twenty bucks for coming out here."

"Oh. Well thanks."

"Yeah. You seem like a nice guy and all. It was nice meeting you. Take care."

"Alright, take care," I said. I sat in Dunkin Donuts for about ten more minutes, scrolling through my iPhone. Then I drove home, feeling like a failure.

Later, I let a frat boy type go down on me in the parking lot of Kinney's. He couldn't get it up, which was somehow my fault, and so he wiggled out of paying.

~~~

About three days after letting Michael fuck me yet again without a condom, the symptoms returned. First it was just discomfort. Then there was serious pain, particularly when I tried to urinate. I'd be doubled over crying, unable to finish. On the fifth day, I woke up with a fever of a hundred and two degrees. That's when I called my friend Jake and asked him to take me to the Civic Center.

Jake was one of several trans friends I had made since returning from California. He was probably the closest to me, though I kept some distance from the entire group. I didn't trust groups of queer friends, with good reason. But I did trust Jake, somewhat. I had found myself estranged from Gabe for unknown reasons. He seemed to be avoiding me.

Jake just seemed like the safest person to call, despite having only known him a few months. He had shown up at CNY for Solidarity and given me a massive energy boost. He was intense, kindhearted, adorably derpy at times, but brooding and serious at others. I related to him in many ways. His passion for social justice struck me immediately as genuine. He was stocky, with blue eyes and long blonde mane that was usually tousled and perhaps un-brushed. He reminded me of a lion. His wardrobe consisted of blue jeans and many black tee shirts, which he usually wore tucked in with a belt, motorcycle boots, and a chest binder. I'd later learn that his mental self-image was very different, and for that reason he hated mirrors. While he exuded masculinity to me, the world interpreted him as androgynous, and it wouldn't be until several more months on testosterone that people stopped calling him "m'am" or occasionally asking whether he was my mom.

We met downtown. It was raining, and I struggled to find parking. Jake came out to meet me at the parking meter, lending his card because I had forgotten my wallet. It wouldn't be the last time he did this for me.

Once inside the clinic, we sat staring at the intake papers. There were of course only two gender options, as usual. I circled neither, and wrote in: *Transgender, from female to male. Female genitalia.* I was learning. I hoped that would eliminate any uncomfortable questions or accusations this time around.

Jake came into the doctor's room with me. The woman I saw this time, Towanna, was very kind. She never even brought up that I was trans, just proceeded to call me by male pronouns even when asking about my vagina. I'm pretty sure she avoided using that term as well.

"Towanna," Jake said, "You're awesome."

"Aw, thanks," she said.

"Could we use you as a point of contact? Not all doctors are as awesome as you. A lot of transgender people in Syracuse have trouble with getting care like this. Would it be okay if we referred people to you?"

"Of course," Towanna said. She gave us her card.

Jake's strength and extraversion in these moments was incredibly attractive to me. It wasn't the first time I had feelings like this for him. We had in common, among many other things, a tremendous sense of urgency. He was turning forty that February, and only now transitioning. He had known he was male from age three, and even named himself Jake. His parents were crazy evangelist Christians, so they tried to exorcize and literally torture it out of him. I knew about his horrible past early on in our friendship. He spoke at Transgender Alliance meeting about his mother's refusal to accept him. To "participate" as she put it.

"Maybe she could talk to my mom," I said, endlessly shy but needing to be helpful. "She was very Catholic, and had trouble with my transition. But she came around eventually."

"No," Jake said, smirking, "She hates Catholics. They're devil worshippers."

"Oh wow," I said, laughing despite myself. "So they are *those* kind of Christians."

"*Yeah*," he said. He was beside Kayla, his partner, on the couch. Kayla was also transgender, and had come out to us first. They had come to the group for her, not Jake. She wasn't okay with his masculine identity though he was supportive of her feminine one.

Trans Alliance was something I started going to only shortly before that. It was a part of my "Return to Syracuse" plan. It didn't really meet my needs. There were several instances and stories that turned me off. The trans woman who lead the group seriously questioned Jake's readiness and right to start hormones – something that was none of her business and caused a serious rift. People also started questioning the legitimacy of my horror stories about Syracuse doctors. It was suggested I should be "silenced" because I was alienating our "allies."

Jake would later tell me how impressed he was with my vulnerability and openness at meetings. That's what made him first fall in love with me. One time an older trans woman, Francis, expressed how she sometimes doubts her gender now that she transitioned. She found dressing up and make-up tiring and just wanted to be a person without so much effort, but worried that if she stopped trying she would be rejected by the community. I assured her that I understood, and shared that sometimes, especially during sex, I identify as a girl. That doesn't make us less trans.

~~~

A few days later I had to go to Urgent Care. I wasn't sure what else to do. I still didn't know what was wrong. I had a fever of over a hundred and two. I felt like I was pissing fire. The discharge was out of control and my insides felt achy and raw.

Jake drove me this time. I couldn't tell anyone else what was happening. In the waiting room, a little boy was crying and his mother kept hitting him and telling him to be quiet.

The intake forms were uncomfortable, but ("Is it OK if I touch you?") less so with Jake's hand on my shoulder.

I can't remember much of this though it was only a month ago. I told a woman in a back room I was transgender. "Oh that's fine!" she said, but it was fake. Later she called me by female pronouns.

I nearly fainted on the way to the exam room. Jake must have helped me. I lied down on the examining table. Somehow I was in a gown and my underwear eventually.

I have a sex addiction. I realized this when I started opening up to Jake. He once had the same problem. He's had a lot of problems, but he's wonderfully kind. He rides a motorcycle- a Honda Rebel. He said I'm an excellent rider. I'd never been on a motorcycle before. He's brilliant at most everything. Brilliant at the things that baffle me-mechanics, math, asserting himself, animal training. He loves the way my back curves and meets my hips. When he says things like this, I feel safe.

"You're beautiful. You're like art." I laugh but it means the world to me. Should this frighten me, that it means so much?

His eyes are light blue. His coloring is similar to Isaac's actually. He's trustworthy when he says these things. I trust him. I let him see me in my girl clothes.

The second female doctor was young and nice enough. She said I needed to do a pelvic exam because if I had gonorrhea I could have an abscess and the only way to know is to poke my cervix and see if it hurts. I panicked. But pelvic exams always hurt, I tried to tell her. I didn't feel like she was listening.

"He has PTSD," Jake said, "And Asperger's. So the pain feels even more intense for him. It won't be an accurate test." I had confided in him these realizations about myself and asked him to be my advocate.

I still didn't feel like the doctor was listening. She went to get a surgeon to talk to me. There was talk about sending me to the ER for intravenous antibiotics. Everything felt out of control.

The surgeon came in. His body was a threat. He was talking too fast and wasn't listening. He told me I had do the pelvic exam. "You've got to relax. Nobody likes it, but you've got to hold still and you can't squirm."

"I don't squirm."

"Okay. But you've just got to relax."

"He's had trauma related to this," Jake said, "He has PTSD."

136

"That doesn't matter," the surgeon said. "You have to just distinguish between real and imagined pain."

Jake snorted.

"I can see you're laughing at me," the surgeon said.

"It doesn't work that way," Jake said. "You aren't listening. He has PTSD. It's going to hurt him whether there's an abscess or not. It won't be an accurate test."

"We see plenty of rape victims," the surgeon said. "It doesn't change the fact that you have to just relax and focus on what is real and what is imaginary."

"It isn't imaginary!" Jake said. Does the name Jacob mean protector? It should.

"It's fine," I mumbled. My voice was higher pitched. I was disappearing. "It's fine, I'll just do it."

"You just can't squirm," the surgeon said. Now everything around me was disappearing too. "Okay?"

"OK." It wasn't okay.

"We'll tell you some jokes to distract you."

"Do not tell me any jokes," I said.

"It's important he feel in control," Jake told the nurse. I could tell she wasn't listening. "It's important you walk him through this and let him know what you're doing each step. You need to have his consent."

"What does that mean?" She asked.

"Consent? It means you need his permission."

I disappeared even more. It hurt everywhere: the opening, the sides, the cervix. It all hurt and I cried out. "Ow! It hurts, stop, it hurts!" and tears streamed down my face. I felt far away from my body and from everything.

Eventually the nurses and doctors left. They left us alone in the room again and I sobbed and shook in the bed.

"Is it OK if I touch you?" Jake whispered.

I nodded. He rubbed my back while I sobbed. "It hurts…"

"I'm so sorry. I shouldn't have let them."

"I didn't want them to. I just said OK to make them go away and stop asking."

"I'm so sorry. Now that I know that about you I won't ever let them do it again."

"I just wanted to be sure I was OK and didn't have an abscess but it didn't matter, it would hurt no matter what…"

"I know…I know…it's OK…"

"Don't let them send me to the ER."

"I won't."

"I'm not going to the ER. I won't go."

"I won't let them send you."

We must have been there five hours. Finally, they said I have an "impressive UTI." They gave me treatment. They ran tests for STDs. While I was peeing in a cup, the original nurse apparently called me by female pronouns. She waited until I wasn't around.

"*He,*" Jake said. "He uses male pronouns."

"Whatever."

"No," a second nurse said, "NOT whatever. He's got enough going on. He doesn't need your shit."

~~~

The next day the fever came back. The itching and the pain was worse. I went to pee and when I pull down my pants, I notice about twenty sores on my pubic mound. I nearly passed out.

I called Jake. He came to get me and we decided it was best to just go to University Internists and my primary care doctor who I stopped seeing because he made me feel guilty last time. *You've got to get your life under control,* he told me. He looked disgusted.

My doctor wasn't available so I had to see another one. "He's very good," the receptionist assured me. If I wasn't so exhausted, I would have laughed. I didn't trust anyone anymore.

Jake came in with me. It was a while before the doctor saw me. He was tall and thin and nondescript, white, probably my father's age or so. He wore glasses and was balding. I told him the story so far while he scribbled things down on a notepad, looking confused. Several times he asked me to repeat what I said or to clarify. I then reached the point where I had to out myself.

"Do you know that I'm transgender?"

Somehow, his silence was hostile. Then— "How would I know that?"

I explained that I thought my doctor may have left notes or something. Some sort of warning. Then I explained that I have a vagina. A very sick, trans-vagina.

"It sounds like herpes," he said. I could tell I had ceased to be a human being in his eyes. "I haven't seen that in years but I'm pretty sure that's what it is." He asked me if any of the sores were open and raw enough that he could take a swab. I said probably not.

"I'll examine it. Lay back and spread your legs."

Holy fucking trigger warning. Don't they train these people at all? What the fuck?

Jake was there though, thankfully. He stood close, behind me, turned away.

The doctor examined me. I felt like a horse being judged at the state fair.

He said he couldn't get a sample unless he cut some of the sores open. I shuddered. No, no, I'll do it.

He got the knife then loomed over me and told me which ones to slice. I did as I was told despite how dizzy and sick I felt. I just wanted to know what was wrong. He then dabbed the blood and puss with a swab. This happened about three times, then he was satisfied.

Jake still stood behind me, facing away to give me privacy. It was very important that he was there though, and he knew it, so he stood close.

"So the real question," the doctor said, turning away from me now with the samples, "is why did you do it?"

"Actually," Jake said, "He doesn't need a lecture. He's been through enough."

<p style="text-align:center">~~~</p>

We were in a hotel room in Portage, Indiana. I was drinking my second raspberry wheat beer and listening to Tracy Chapman, smoking an electronic cigarette. The nicotine vapor tasted sweet and stung my throat a little. Jake was in the king size bed, typing on his laptop. Outside the window the land was flat, with long dry grasses and a warehouse in the distance. The grass moved in waves with the prairie winds.

"Is that a prairie?" I asked Jake, pointing out the window. He laughed.

"Not really."

"What makes something prairie?"

I don't remember what he said.

Jake and I have done a lot of travelling these past three months that we've been together.

We're here in Indiana because his son is at a camp for model aeronomics. There have also been the trips to Philadelphia with the Mazzoni Bus. We transport transgender people from Syracuse who aren't getting the health care they need— trans people including ourselves. This is a big part of CNY for Solidarity's mission. Eventually we'd like to have a satellite clinic here in Syracuse. I don't want to see people go through what I've had to, whether to get on hormones, STD tests, a therapist, or just basic care. I'm not sure why, but our efforts have made us a lot of enemies in the local LGBT community. Particularly the T community. That's a long story though, and best left for another volume of work.

I've been living with Jake since his partner split up with him unexpectedly. First, as a supportive friend, now as his partner. We're on the southwest side of Syracuse, in a house that inhabits too many people: several trans men and women, me, and Jake and his fourteen year old son, Xander. It isn't exactly working for me, but I'm making the best of it until we find better arrangements.

We went to Lake Michigan in the evening. There were factories lining the waters, but the sunset was beautiful. The water was as cold as the ocean in Santa Cruz, but Jake walked in anyway, shirt, shorts, chest-binder and all. He walked out far, until the water reached his chest. Far away, he kind of resembled Jesus for some reason. I watched him from the shore and smoked my vapor cigarette. I felt calm.

We spent the next day in the small town of Chesterton, sipping iced coffee and sitting at a bistro table on the sidewalk. We both used that time to write. Jake also does some creative writing, among many other things, though he doesn't consider himself an especially creative person. He used to train dogs and horses and even birds. He once had a pet crow that he rescued. He's been thinking about dog training again to make a living. Back home in Syracuse, we've been rescuing baby skunks from our violent neighbors. We catch them in cardboard boxes and transport them to a secret location outside the city.

He's a vegetarian, too.

I was using the bathroom at the café in Chesterton when I realized how close we were to James Dean's hometown and grave. We drove to Fairmount the next day, with Xander in the back seat, unsure who James Dean even was. There were cornfields and windmills as far as the eye could see.

Fairmount was dinky and economically depressed. A ghost town, with nothing but antique stores and a museum we skipped over. Jake took my picture at the cemetery, by Dean's grave. There was a couple there, visiting from Texas. They eyed us with distrust.

I don't know what's coming next. Jake came into my life seemingly out of nowhere. We were friends for a while, working together on CNY for Solidarity. He was there for me when no one else was. Then one night, his partner left him, he asked me to come over to a bonfire. I ended up staying the night, and I've lived there ever since. Maybe it sounds fucked up, but it's working. We've both been abused and misunderstood. We deserve a break. We deserve each other.

We take the motorcycle places in the state. Ithaca, the Adirondacks, isolated riversides where we drink and swim nude and have incomprehensibly wonderful times. I swam out and lay on a smooth rock. "This is heaven," I kept telling him, my bottom half submerged in the refreshing, dark water.

Now I'm in downtown Syracuse. Everything is swirling and I have trouble keeping it straight. Different parts of me experience different moments. The narrative is fuzzy and disjointed. There are some things I'm starting to know:

1.   I am recovering from sex addiction.

2.   I have dissociative identity disorder

3.   I have Aspergher's.

4.   I have a drinking problem.

5.   I was abused as a child, though I can't remember it all.

6.   I was abused as a teen, and it counted as such.

7.   I was abused as a young adult, and it wasn't my fault.

8.   I have post-traumatic stress disorder.

9.   My genders are complicated and not as simple as "trans man." I don't regret my decision, but I am lowering my testosterone some. I'm experimenting. I want to be more physically androgynous. At least right now.

10.   The more I let my transfemininity show, the more dangerous the world seems. But it is important I express it if I want to stop self-destructing.

11.   I love Jake and I can trust him. He loves me and he can trust me too.

I'm wearing leopard print skinny blue jeans and a purple tiger striped top. I am on the corner of Jefferson and Salina. Men aren't fem here. Not even the gay men. I stand out, like irreverent prey. But I refuse to be prey. Men pass and I wonder, do they recognize me? It's hard, but I am going to finish this book. I'm going to complete it, even if it's unclear what I'm trying to say. I need to say it.

Syracuse is busy today, almost like a real city. I find the noise and chaos to be comforting. The beat is inspiring. I feel alive and a part of

144

things. I don't know what's coming next. I don't need to know. Right now, I'm just happy to be out of the suburbs, and out of my parents' house. I'll stick with Jake. He doesn't solve everything, or perhaps anything—but he certainly doesn't make life worse. We'll keep travelling, exploring, adapting, making ends meet. And maybe, just maybe, the worst is over.

Afterword By Evelyn Deshane

In Truman Capote's award winning novel *In Cold Blood*, he discusses the murders of a Kansas family that he read in the newspaper. The initial article peaked Capote's interest and led him on a long road trip to investigate the case along with his childhood friend, Harper Lee (you may have heard of her and her book *To Kill A Mocking Bird*). What they found ended up in this long, page turning book. But this book, though based on very real events and inspired by curiosity, is not *quite* true.

Truman Capote called *In Cold Blood* a nonfiction novel. While he was not the first to use this term, he certainly popularized it.[1] The term nonfiction novel embraces the limits in what we can remember, recall, and retell about our own lives. This term embraces our own fallibility as humans with complex emotions and even more complicated memories and personal histories. Though the stories that we tell about our lives may feel very true, when compared to other's perspectives, case reports, or the same news headlines that peaked Capote's curiosity, we may find that all that we knew about ourselves is a long lie. When we think we know cannot be truly tested. Our memories are not scientific facts. But they do make a good story, and it's that good story that compels Capote to keep talking, though the image of Kansas may not be quite the same.

I bring up Capote's subtle nod to the truth but-not-quite-the-truth because I think this is important to keep in mind when reading Elliott DeLine's *Show Trans*. The veracity of his words is not one hundred percent. "The truth is," DeLine writes within the first thirty pages. "I can't capture everything in my life. It's impossible. Memory is fuzzy." These lines seem to repeat themselves again and again. He is very aware that his memory is shaky, is not quite all there, and yet, he has chosen to tell the story anyway. It is not the factual truth of this account that matters – and this is what readers need to consider the most. These are DeLine's thoughts, actions, and recollections on certain events in his life. His story is important not because it is true, but because *he* is the one who told it.

---

[1] Geoffrey of Monmouth was popular in this genre around the 12th century.

~~~

In his past work, *Refuse* and *I Know Very Well How I Got My Name*, DeLine has fictionalized his past and created characters from real life moulds. Jack Kerouac, the fiction author from the 1950s, was known for doing this in his novel *On The Road*. When pressed in interviews after Kerouac's death, many of the iconic writer's associates stated that he wanted to build a "mythology" out of the time and the people he knew.[2] While Dean Moriarty and Sal Paradise are two very different people than their real life counterparts Jack Kerouac and his friend Neal Cassady, Kerouac was successful in his mission as an author. Just ask any twenty-something hipster in a coffee bar who still clutches Kerouac as if he were a God.

In the case of *Show Trans*, I see Isaac and Elliott – and their fictional monikers Dean and Colin – as the great stand-ins for Dean Moriarty and Sal Paradise. The great road trip which spans most of DeLine's text, from Syracuse to San Francisco and back again, only makes this comparison in my mind stronger. Isaac, and especially Elliott, are heading out on the road to seek the "mad ones" of their generation. In fact, take that quotation by Kerouac and replace "mad" for something like "queer" and I think that summarizes DeLine's whole text:

> They danced down the streets like dingledodies, and I shambled after as I've been doing all my life after people who interest me, because the only people for me are the mad ones, the ones who are mad to live, mad to talk, mad to be saved, desirous of everything at the same time, the ones who never yawn or say a commonplace thing, but burn, burn, burn like fabulous yellow roman candles exploding like spiders across the stars and in the middle you

[2] See *The Source* (1999) documentary for an in-depth look at the oral storytelling of Jack Kerouac and The Beats mythology.

see the blue centerlight pop and everybody goes "Awww!" (*On The Road*, Chapter One).

More than just a neat correlation, I see Elliott DeLine (the writer, not the character) as the equivalent of Kerouac for the queer crowd. The problem with Kerouac, as many scholars before me have said, is that at the end of the day, he was a repressed white boy who clung onto ideals instead of actually striving for change. At the end of his life, Kerouac drank himself to death and thought himself a failure. And the people who clutch his books as if they were gospels often fall under the same error of his ways. They are white men, writing about manic pixie dreams girls, and hoping that someone will think their precious thoughts wonderful. There have been a million books and movies about this topic already. See *Garden State*, *Looking for Alaska*, *Elizabethtown*, *Almost Famous*. Also, notice how most of these examples also have a road trip or a return to home involved in their plots? The road narrative begs for white, middle class guys who have the time to think about their life and deem it worthy enough to write down.

In some ways, DeLine is doing exactly what Kerouac did – talking about his life, his failures, and making himself into a confessional martyr. But how many of those books and films have involved *transgender* men doing the confessing? How many have involved discussions of queer sexuality?

My guess is none. Even Kerouac could not quite get out his repressed love and desire for Cassady. Though more road novels with queer characters at the forefront are more being written, such as Imogen Binnie's *Nevada* which centers around a transgender woman, there is still a pressing need to counteract every kid with a Starbucks cup of coffee who quotes Kerouac or Bukowski without thinking. Because their voices will be heard. They have already been heard. But people like Elliott DeLine or Imogen Binnie will not always be remembered, even if they are heard.

~~~

The transgender narrative is often structured as an "inward journey." The 'true' or 'authentic' gender is discovered, there is a revelation of new identity, and a healing of trauma. These things happen through therapy; through talking and telling stories. In other words, they can be quite passive. They can take place in confinement – which transgender people have often found themselves in as well.[3] And if these narratives do not use the go-to of confessing and internal struggles, then their narrative structure often conforms around the medical institution and surgery.

In a recent conversation with Katie Couric, Laverne Cox stated that by focusing on the surgical aspect of transitioning, "we don't focus on the lived realities of oppression and discrimination." We also "objectify" the transgender body. I believe Cox's statements to be correct. If every single story about a group of people (transgender people make up around 1% of the US population[4]) focuses on an invasive and painful procedure that reduces a body to its mere ability to conform to certain notions of what "correct" genitals are supposed to look like – then storytelling for this group of people can get pretty depressing pretty quickly.

In another keynote address, Laverne Cox also stated that medical care for transgender people is not an elective – it is a necessity.[5] And again, the wonderful actress of *Orange Is The New Black,* is correct. Surgery is needed and beneficial to a transgender person's identity. But it is not the be-all or end-all of their lives. There is more to transgender narratives than talk therapy and waiting lists for medical care. The road that begins after surgery is just as important – if not more – than the road that got the person there.

Show Trans discusses that road after surgery in great detail. It's a book largely about sexuality as much as it is about transgender status. With DeLine's frank discussion, he deconstructs every last category

---

[3] See the documentary *Cruel and Unusual* for the abysmal conditions of transgender people in the prison system. Also note Laverne Cox's forthcoming documentary about CeCe McDonald and her experiences in the prison system.

[4] Stat from transequality.org.

[5] *Creating Change Speech*, February 2014.

of transgender storytelling and provides a new space to have such discussions. In short, it's a book about DeLine's relationships with other men – and the gay community's need to adapt and change.

DeLine and other transsexual bodies who have had surgery, but still lack a phallus, pose a threat to some men in the gay community. More than that, there is another strong border between what is straight and what is gay in most LGBT circles (also known pejoratively as the GGGG community). There is very little room for anything in-between in most male sexuality. Either you're gay and hate vaginas and or you're a man who thinks that pussy is pussy. These attitudes are not an essential part about being a 'man,' but these sentiments are bred into our culture. When actors like Alan Cumming have to try and convince interviewers and his audience that he is bisexual, even if he is married to a man, then there is an issue with sexuality and its multiplicities in North America.[6] When given a body that represents something in-between, the borders of identities become hard to decipher and therefore policed more.

This is DeLine's attempt to find his "nationality" within this bordered space, and also reject the term all together. As he has stated in a recent Huffington Post interview, "I don't identify as gay." For DeLine, "I think if everybody stopped looking at sexuality as a black-and-white kind of thing, stopped looking at gender as a black-and-white kind of thing" then sexuality and those who wish to live between its borders would be a lot more welcome at home.

~~~

In Jay Prosser's work *Second Skins*, he discusses the transgender body using language usually reserved for nationalism. He states the importance of "coming home" to the body after the final surgery. From this perspective, Prosser argues that many transgender narratives align with diasporic narratives. Each represents the feeling of displacement in a land (or body) that used to be familiar and the uncanny feeling of walking into a new landscape and trying to find a proper road home.

---

[6] From an article on *The Huffington Post*, dated 12/17/2013.

DeLine's builds on Prosser's basic idea of coming home and he pushes it a step further. Instead of longing for the body/home of the proper gender, DeLine writes about the desire for the home/body of someone else who understands. DeLine's travels take him from his home in Syracuse, NY to the brightly coloured graffiti'd walls of San Francisco and his former lover's arms. Their bodies, when pressed together in one of the most moving scenes, both contain the same matching scars.

> I nodded, feeling an ache in my limbs that seemed to underscore my timid longing. I put my arms around his neck and he circled his around my waist. His upper body was much broader than my own and I loved the way he felt—the way our flat, scarred chests pressed together through our tee shirts, the way his hands felt as they rubbed my back, the way he gave me a tight squeeze of reassurance.

This is where DeLine pushes the standard transgender narrative to another step. It is no longer a mirror that DeLine is looking at to find himself, alone. Instead he is looking for recognition inside another person. That is why this book is important. Love is part of the human condition, part of a universal story that everyone can relate to. But coming from DeLine, a queer trans person at this particular period in time, this story is more moving than a thousand *Garden States* or *Almost Famous*. This book is a road trip where one person tries to figure out how he feels in love while also maintaining the person he always thought he was.

The thing about identity is that it involves this process of recognition. We are not island, in the very Shakespearean sense of the term.[7] We need others, not to tell us who we are, but to confirm what we already know about ourselves. It's only when we trust that the person on the other side of the table understands what we're saying that we feel comfortable enough to say it. This is why asking for pronouns and

---

[7] Reference to *The Tempest*, where old Prospero tries to shelter himself on an island, but is proved to be the fool of the play.

using proper names and gendered terms are important. Our identities are discursive, but they also involve recognition and confirmation from other people. When that sense of recognition is there, we are able to fall in love.

In a lot of ways, this is a nonfiction novel about a broken love story that must be written in order to move away from it. In other ways, it's a cutting and private look at the life of a transgender person who dares to be sexual. It's a study into a new mode of gay culture and new concerns that the community needs to address. It's also, at its heart, a road novel that continues to bounce back and forth between two coasts, trying to find the proper place to belong. It's a novel about being split in two, sometimes quite literally, and so deep it leaves matching scars.

~~~

Thomas Wolfe once said, "You can't go home again." He said this, I believe, to remove all the romanticism, sentimentality, and idealism that we keep around our childhood homes. Nostalgia represents a longing for the past that is not quite there. The word itself is made from the two Greek compound words for "homecoming" and "ache." We ache when we come home, because like Capote told us in so many words, we write a nonfiction novel in our minds about where we were from. We embellish the characters. We make the hero greater than he may have been on the surface. And we make the road home the most important one.

Thomas Wolfe saw this as something to be avoided. But for some, like DeLine or other transgender people who may have never been allowed to experience their home, going back can be a good experience. In order to understand where you come from, you need to leave. And you need to go back home in order to know why it's important to leave again. Identity is not a fixed state and therefore, I think some bodies yearn for constant motion. DeLine represents that constant motion, especially in this book. The car and the road is then the perfect metaphor for this new way of looking at identity and relationships. Nothing is permanent, but maybe there can be some good songs to listen to while on the road, and small things – like open mics and book readings– to keep the journey interesting.

 In many transgender narratives, the book ends with surgery – with that act of coming home. But for DeLine, he knows that home is not the last stop, and definitely not the last book to be written on this topic.

About The Author:

"Though DeLine is only 24, with Refuse and I Know Very Well How I Got My Name, his is already a major contribution to queer literature. Like so many of the classic gay and lesbian novels from the earlier part of the 20th century, these works are sure, years from now, to enjoy wider readership and recognition as pioneering examples of transgender writing. Moreover, DeLine's well-crafted storytelling and skill at cultivating voice prove that, far from being a niche genre, transgender narratives by transgender authors are a welcome and still underrepresented presence in contemporary fiction today."

-Jameson Fitzpatrick, *Kirkus Reviews*

Elliott DeLine (born 1988) is a transgender writer and activist from Syracuse, NY. He is the author of the novel *Refuse* and the novella *I Know Very Well How I Got My Name.* His work has been featured in the *Modern Love* essay series of *The New York Times, The Collection: Short Fiction from the Transgender Vanguard,* and *Original Plumbing Magazine.* He is a founder and vice president of the nonprofit CNY for Solidarity, Inc., and the general coordinator of Queer Mart, an LGBTQ arts and crafts fair. Elliott currently lives in Syracuse, NY.

For more information and other books, visit
elliottdeline.com

Special thanks to the patrons who helped make this book a reality. As an independent artist, I am entirely dependent on the continued generosity and loyalty of my readers. Much love and appreciation to each of you.

Aine Ni Cheallaigh
Alex Smith
Andrew Molloy
Dylan Suttles
Erica Kenny
Ellis Locke
Jameson Fitzpatrick
Linda Kirbow
Logan Walker
Nicole Cotty
Nora Olsen
Robin Lawlor
Sandra King
Terri and Vince Cook
Tristan Collins

Special thanks also to Evelyn Deshane for her eloquent "afterword."

And especially Joseph Mudge, for all his time spent formatting the texts and photos in this book. I love you.

Sincerely,

Elliott

Self portrait at age 25

Made in the USA
Middletown, DE
10 June 2015